Taming the Standards

Taming the Standards

A COMMONSENSE APPROACH TO
HIGHER STUDENT ACHIEVEMENT, K–12

Janet Hurt

HEINEMANN
Portsmouth, NH

Heinemann
A division of Reed Elsevier Inc.
361 Hanover Street
Portsmouth, NH 03801–3912
www.heinemann.com

Offices and agents throughout the world

The author and publisher wish to thank those who have generously given permission to reprint borrowed material:

Figures 3–1, 3–2, and 4–1 used by permission of the Kentucky Department of Education.

Figures 3–3, 6–1, and 6–2 used by permission of the Logan County Board of Education, Russellville, Kentucky.

Figures 5–1 and 5–4 used by permission of science teacher Bethany Hill.

Library of Congress Cataloging-in-Publication Data
Hurt, Janet.
     Taming the standards : a commonsense approach to higher student achievement, K–12 / Janet Hurt.
          p. cm.
     Includes bibliographical references.
     ISBN 0-325-00592-3 (alk. paper)
     1. Education—Standards—United States. 2. Academic achievement—United States. I. Title.
     LB3060.83.H87 2003
     379.1'58'0973—dc21   2003011648

Editor: Danny Miller
Production: Vicki Kasabian
Cover design: Lisa Fowler
Typesetter: Tom Allen, Pear Graphic Design
Manufacturing: Steve Bernier

Printed in the United States of America on acid-free paper
07 06 05 04 03 RRD 1 2 3 4 5

For my mother, Ruth Bain Lanphear

CONTENTS

ACKNOWLEDGMENTS

There are times in your life when you meet people without foreseeing how they will impact your life and your learning. I am truly blessed because some of these special people have come into my life.

Linda Hargan, Christie Maloney, and Amy Awbrey from the Collaborative for Teaching and Learning in Louisville, Kentucky, are three of these people, as well as Christina Cocek, whose path I thankfully crossed several years ago. They provide me a forum for debate and learning. Because of my great admiration and respect for them personally and professionally for their work in assisting teachers and schools, I am honored to call them my friends, colleagues, and partners in learning.

Authors Rose Taylor and Ivan Hannel have also touched me in special ways. They both gave untold hours to help make this book possible. Rose pushed me to write by being my writing partner in the early days of this book. Ivan painstakingly read my manuscript and provided much needed advice as this book was taking shape. Their excitement for my journey was obvious and genuine, and I will be forever grateful for their encouragement and support.

A special friend and fabulous educational consultant, Sylvia Abell, provided her expertise in editing and by providing feedback during the writing process. Her assistance provided clarity to the organization and flow of this book.

I have been extremely fortunate to have Danny Miller as my editor. He would often say things that unleashed my passion and sent me scrambling to my computer to fire off a long email to him responding to his comments and questions. I always imagined him sitting at his desk with a smirk on his face thinking that he had accomplished his goal. I finally realized that his job was to encourage me, yet keep the passion for my work ignited. He asked provocative questions and guided me to understand that the process of writing is about unleashing words in a truthful and straightforward manner.

The Logan County Board of Education has provided the springboard for much of my work. Not everyone is fortunate to work with the caliber of people with whom I work. Teachers in this district have contributed to this book at every level. Without the teachers from all of the schools, my growth and learning would stagnate. Additionally, I have a wonderful superintendent, Marshall Kemp, who supports my work within and outside of our school district. His trust and faith in my daily work has provided me the courage to reach beyond the surface. My coworkers such as Associate Superintendent Tommy Perdue continue to provide a safety net when I venture off the beaten path looking for better ways. Finally, the members of the Logan County Board of Education continuously challenge me by having high expectations for everyone in our district. This professional challenge has stretched and nurtured my learning.

My wonderful family has rallied around me and provided support in this journey of learning. My mother, Ruth, and stepfather, Roy, were my role models of lifelong learners. Until they both passed away, they continued to learn. My mother was an educator and author, but my stepfather also epitomized lifelong learning. In fact, he was buried with his favorite book. Their legacy continues to influence the decisions, choices, and values of their children, my siblings, David, Jane, and Lisa, and their grandchildren, who continue to embrace their values about education.

My children all pitched in to provide me the necessary time to work with schools and teachers and then to write about that learning. My four-year-old daughter, Sydney, stayed busy by stapling papers together before placing them in the trash; my oldest daughter, Alison, babysat and monitored the stapling processes; and my son, John, assisted by providing much of the entertainment.

Finally, this book could not have been written without the assistance and support given to me by a special person, my husband, Mike Hurt. He not only assisted me in facilitating many workshops, but he also assisted behind the scenes when he engaged me in regular conversations and played the devil's advocate. The repartee between us could become quite intense, but it kept me grounded in what is important. He supports me in many ways from making suggestions, conducting workshops, and traveling with me across the country to doing the little things that allow me the necessary time to devote to my work. He is a visionary principal, yet he is grounded and practical. I want to say thank you for being who you are—a dedicated educator, a great dad, a wonderful husband, and my best friend.

INTRODUCTION

Looking at Standards Differently

Taming the Standards: A Commonsense Approach to Higher Student Achievement, K–12 is a book based on the work of hundreds of teachers who were working to align their curriculum into something more than just a list of content and skills. Through their work, I have recorded the steps for the process of building an aligned curriculum system that is grounded in practical application. Standards are examined and used in this process to prod students to higher levels of learning.

Although there are many books written about the pitfalls of the standards movement in the United States, few books offer an alternative for improving the system. The process explained in this book is not dependent on just the standards that are rich with conceptual meaning: it addresses how teachers can transform ineffective standards into more powerful learning for the benefit of students.

States are providing standards to local school districts and more and more states are mandating their use by aligning state assessment to them. Our challenge as educators is to find a way to use those standards so that students will score higher on state assessments and will benefit from the use of higher level concepts that are either embedded deeply within or beyond the standards.

We have an obligation to use the standards to meet state mandates, but since many standards are less effective than others, it is sometimes a difficult task. Using many standards as they are written is often no better than using the old-fashioned "skills lists" that were so popular a decade ago. We must make our standards better, but not so that we can teach them; rather, we must guide students through them and beyond in order to provide our students a rich foundation.

How Did I Get Here?

My mother was the first person in her family to graduate from college. Although her mother was not an educated woman, she instilled in my mother the belief that education broadens one's perspectives and opens doors that otherwise might remain forever closed to a poor Texas girl. My grandmother insisted that my mother get an education and read as much as possible so that one day my mother could move away from the run-down shacks located on their relatives' farms.

The first and best example of someone who loved to learn was my mother. She planned for the future of her children by setting high expectations for us. Her childhood molded her style of mothering, and she succeeded in making education important to each of us. Maybe because of or maybe in spite of that, she became a teacher who chaired the English and the Foreign Language departments at her school and later became a school administrator. She claimed that she had a good life because of education.

Her influence on my work is evident everywhere, but especially in examining the standards. Before she died, we had many discussions around the merits of the standards movement. She encouraged me to look beyond standards because there was so much more to life than learning a list of things that someone else labeled important. Two weeks before she died, I told her that I had decided to write a book that outlined a step-by-step process for taming the standards. Her legacy lives on in this book. It is through her encouragement that I learned the truth—learning opens doors, but it is up to us to look behind them, evaluate the merits of their content, and to reach for a higher meaning.

My first year as a principal, I faked it. I pretended to know what I didn't know. I would walk into the building every morning thinking, "Do the teachers know what a fake I am? Can they tell that I am an imposter?" I knew very little about how to evaluate teachers and even less about curriculum. Teachers came to me with exciting ideas that they had found or thought of and my response was always the same, "You are the experts in your classrooms so if you feel that this is a good idea, you should try it." This response served two purposes. It shielded my lack of knowledge from the teachers' view, and allowed the teachers to feel that I had confidence in their abilities. If I had uttered another word, I would have demonstrated my ignorance.

I had taught second, sixth, seventh, and eighth grades, and served as a guidance counselor and as an assistant principal, but nothing had prepared me for the hot fire of high-stakes accountability that would burn my heels. Even more worrisome than that was having teachers look to me to lead them through that fire.

I made a conscious decision during my second year: I decided that the students and staff deserved a principal who cared enough to learn what good teaching and an aligned curriculum looked like. I finally admitted to the staff that I did not have answers. Luckily, they took my hand and allowed me to walk with them on this journey of learning.

Looking back, I recognize that without the experience of serving as the principal of a school that had such a forgiving staff, I would still be hiding behind my pretense. Therefore, this journey is also about the teachers and staff members who embraced my desire and who challenged me to think differently.

A Personal Learning Journey

Maybe the first time I realized I was making progress was the day I was reading a professional book and thought to myself, "This author does not know what it is really like out here in the trenches. She needs to go back to reality and ground herself in practical application." Immediately it dawned on me that I had just disagreed with an expert. What a revelation for me since I had always been compliant and in awe of those leaders in our field. That revelation plays in my mind every time I encounter a teacher who believes that authors of textbooks and resource manuals are gurus, and every time I see teachers who clutch these materials as if they were holy.

Because of high-stakes accountability, several teachers and I began discussing the best way to align our curriculum so that we would not have to worry about whether we were addressing what was tested, and we could concentrate more of our time on implementing current research-based strategies.

In the beginning, we had so many failures that it seemed we would never find a method that worked well. We created alignment documents that were too lengthy, too brief, too confusing, too cumbersome, too rigid, too skills-based, too broad, and too narrow to be useful. But at least we were creating them, which was more than most districts around us at that time were doing. Because of this, I began to receive invitations to assist other schools in developing alignment documents.

Because we saw a need, the teachers joined me in throwing out days and days of work and patiently beginning again and again in an effort to find a way to hold ourselves more accountable for using standards to increase student achievement. This process repeated itself until most of us knew hundreds of standards by heart.

Many teachers and I discussed and examined issues around alignment, the use of questions, and higher concepts that we wanted to incorporate into our instruction. Kathy Dotson was one teacher who did not mind debating the issues of alignment. She and I would spend endless hours looking at questions and concepts to determine what made them worthy of our students.

Other teachers often joined into the conversations, but some were wearing their resources on their sleeves. A few cried when I voiced my initial opinion that textbooks and resource manuals should not drive our instruction. I believed that if textbooks and resources could replace the process of alignment and good planning, then all students should be reaching higher levels than they were because we had been using those documents for a long, long time. No one holds the only answer, but teachers who are closest to their students hold a better answer than someone across the country.

Instead of enjoying a respite in the evenings when I was home, I found myself deep into conversations with my husband, who is a principal, around what we could do to help students achieve at higher levels without overburdening teachers. We spent many hours every week trying to solve the problems in education. Eventually, we had a meeting of the minds and began conducting some workshops together. We also began exploring ways to make teachers' jobs easier. Ultimately, we designed a software program for our schools, Lesson Plan Xpress, which is now owned by the Collaborative for Teaching and Learning in Louisville, Kentucky. We learned a lot together, and he too has left his fingerprints, his experience, and his expertise on the process of taming the standards.

In one school district, I conducted a districtwide workshop for middle school teachers who were interested in examining their standards more closely. To demonstrate the numerous interpretations that we all have of standards, I wrote one standard on the board and asked groups of teachers to brainstorm what was important for students to know about that standard. I listed the responses from each of the nine groups as findings were reported. Every response was different proving that we all, including experts, bring our own thinking and interpretations to standards. Teachers were shocked and frightened. How could one standard cause so much confusion? After all, these teachers had been teaching that standard for years. If that happened in one district, imagine the confusion when we depend on people from other places to interpret our standards and tell us what is important. Have they examined our state assessments, too? Most teachers are professionals who prefer to make that call for themselves.

The process outlined in this book was not a sudden discovery. Most of it was learned in pieces from hundreds of teachers in many different schools. In one workshop, a teacher asked if it was okay for her to bundle her standards in a way that I had tried before with little success. I explained my many unsuccessful attempts, but left the final decision up to her. She proceeded to use the method that I had not been fond of and appeared to be doing well with it. In fact, I was beginning to reevaluate my position. However, later she asked me how she was going to complete the next step, and I explained that she had just hit one of the same walls that I had encountered using that method. We worked her through the dilemma, but she informed me that I should have just told her not to use that method. She was right, but by using it, she reaffirmed for me again that the methods in this book are based on practical experience from teachers struggling to find answers to curriculum alignment and using standards to positively impact student achievement.

While I believe that standards are one way that we as educators can hold ourselves accountable, I also recognize the shortcomings of many of the standards that are mandated to us. Many standards are substandard. Nevertheless, we cannot ignore standards because students' assessment results are often tied directly to them.

To tame your standards, you will use standards to teach to a higher level. I did not say you would teach your standards, rather I said you would *use* them. In this process, we look through our standards and locate the deeper meaning within them or beyond them to help students make sense of standards, which are often just a list of content and skills attached to some verbs.

So how do we use standards? If loftier concepts are not embedded within the standards, we must reach beyond, beneath, and behind them to find what is important for students to learn. We ask:

- What is so important about this standard that students should know?
- What is within, beyond, beneath, and behind standards that makes them important?
- How can I use this standard to teach students about something that is more durable?
- How can I use standards to help students transfer learning to other facets of their lives and to the world around them?

These and other questions will guide the process of taming our standards.

I have chosen to write a book based on my experiences in providing assistance to schools and teachers who were struggling to manage their curriculum. Each group of teachers gave me new insight into the real world of standards—the good, the bad, and the indifferent. Standards can be managed and tamed so that they become a vehicle to assist students in achieving at higher levels. Standards are not the target—we only use them to guide students to higher levels of learning.

How Is This Book Organized?

Each chapter is organized around the step being addressed, scaffolding learning from the previous chapter and spiraling into the next chapter. A discussion of the specific steps is illustrated by a middle school example that weaves through the chapters. Real-life examples of application in a school setting are provided. The Pitfalls to Avoid in each chapter are shared to make your success easier. Each chapter closes with terms that will promote a common vocabulary among the readers and that are critical for deeper understanding. Those wanting to pursue the study of the concepts and topics from the chapters in more depth and the strategies of collaboration will want to note the selections in Further Reading.

How Do I Begin?

The steps in this book are best executed by a collaborative team of teachers working together, but one teacher working through one content area can successfully tame the standards, too. Teachers begin this process by examining standards to identify the umbrella concepts embedded within and beyond their standards. This process gives empowerment to those who know the needs of their students and how to address them.

It is my hope that this book will allow educators to have a smooth journey through creating an aligned curriculum system, from examining standards to examining student work. Experience has been a bumpy road. The naysayers even threw a few rocks in the beginning thinking that the work was just a pet project, rather than a long-term commitment to student learning. But thanks to the teachers who persevered, we learned to be firmly grounded in practical application. Through the experience, reflection, and continued growth of many teachers, I offer you a path to success.

Since this process challenges teachers to think differently about standards and about the design and implementation of standards-based units, I suggest reading the entire book prior to beginning the process. This will allow time for internalizing and reflecting on new learning and will provide a view of the end product before the first step in taken. Journey on and join the hundreds of teachers who have walked before you.

Terms to Remember

Collaborative team: Two or more educators working for a common purpose in a culture of trust.

Empowerment: Giving the responsibility of design, implementation, accountability, and reward to others.

Standards: Identified processes, knowledge, skills, or concepts that students are expected to know, do, and apply as assessed by state requirements.

Umbrella concepts: Big ideas or concepts identified from the standards under which standards, skills, and knowledge can be bundled.

Further Reading

Blase, J., and J. Blase. 2002. *Empowering Teachers: What Successful Principals Do.* Thousand Oaks, CA: Corwin Press.

Deal, T. E., and K. D. Peterson. 1999. *Shaping School Culture: The Heart of Leadership.* San Francisco: Jossey-Bass.

DuFour, R., and R. Eaker. 1998. *Professional Learning Communities at Work: Best Practices for Enhancing Student Achievement.* Bloomington, IN: National Educational Service.

Falk, B. 2000. *The Heart of the Matter: Using Standards and Assessment to Learn.* Portsmouth, NH: Heinemann.

Ohanian, S. 1999. *One Size Fits Few.* Portsmouth, NH: Heinemann.

Wilde, S. 2002. *Testing and Standards: A Brief Encyclopedia.* Portsmouth, NH: Heinemann.

Williams, R. D., and R. Taylor. 2002. *Leading with Character to Improve Student Achievement.* Chapel Hill, NC: Character Development.

1
Uncovering Concepts
Umbrella and Content Specific

I use this process as a way of critically looking at the connections across the curriculum and as a means of concentrating my instruction so I can take students past the knowledge level and into the application and synthesis level. It ties everything together that used to be disjointed into something meaningful for students.

—Penny Wallace, fifth-grade teacher,
Morgantown Elementary School

Time is an elusive commodity. We never have enough of it. A friend of mine says she only works to buy other people's time. She buys the time of the farmers who grow her food, builders who build her home, dry cleaners who starch and press her clothes, and hairdressers who cut her hair. Educators are in a particularly precarious situation because they are expected to stay abreast of new research, learn how to implement new instructional and assessment techniques, and teach all day. Planning time is minimal, certainly not long enough to do all they need to do. Teachers have no time, yet they are bound by high expectations. Even professional development time is often out of their control. And the typical American school year of 180 days is not enough time to address all the standards in all subject areas for which each teacher is responsible.

During the past decade, the standards movement in the United States has moved across the country until virtually every state has state standards. State departments of education have outlined what students are expected to understand and packaged those expectations as standards. Some of these standards are exhaustive and encompass a broad range of concepts while other standards are extremely narrow and written as discrete skills. There are standards requiring students to perform low-level tasks such as "list the names of early explorers" and other standards nudging students to investigate the "why" behind the list. Nevertheless, all are standards. Each state has adopted its own name for these standards such as Florida's Sunshine

State Standards, Colorado's Model Content Standards, and Idaho's Achievement Standards. Sometimes it is difficult to find the commonality from state to state when comparing the names of the standards and the styles in which the standards are written. Most state standards are based on the standards developed and promoted by the content area national professional organizations like the National Council of Teachers of English (NCTE) and the National Council of Teachers of Mathematics (NCTM). Even when states draft their standards from these documents, it is often hard to see the linkage and commonality between them.

Standards are usually handed down from state departments of education. Teachers frequently feel no ownership, and they certainly do not have the time to assess the quality of the standards. The truth is that some states have developed standards that are laced with higher-level ideas from nudging students to view history through multiple perspectives to other states that advocate standards that are so skill-based that it is difficult to find a higher level of thinking within them. Standards by their very definition imply some set measure, but I challenge you to find measure in a uniform application across the nation or within many states. The fact is that many standards are less than effective.

Standards that are awkward or cumbersome result in teachers avoiding them until the arm of accountability reaches out. Teachers are left with little choice of whether to address standards since state assessments are usually tied directly to their mastery. Teachers are under intense pressure to teach the standards so that students will score well on state tests, and in many states rewards and sanctions are imposed depending upon the incremental performance levels of students.

In the world of high-stakes accountability, the reality is that teachers are forced to address the standards and acknowledge their importance. With time ticking away, most teachers have neither the time nor the inclination to debate the quality of their standards because they are too busy trying to address them. The good news is that states usually do not mandate how to organize or address the standards, which allows teachers the liberty to take back some control.

We begin the journey with teachers who decided to bring their standards to life by looking within and beyond them for all the possibilities. Standards that are lacking in higher-level thinking can be enhanced by looking beyond them and asking, Why is this standard important for students to learn and how can I, as the teacher, see beyond the discrete content or skill to find a deeper meaning to guide students to higher levels?

Teachers not only have the right to improve their standards, they have a responsibility to find a deeper meaning in standards by using their common sense and professional judgment to sprinkle the standards with connectors, purpose, and relevance.

Through high-stakes accountability and the necessity for all students to achieve at high levels, schools and districts are recognizing that the best instructional and assessment practices in the world will not produce measurable gains in student achievement if instruction is not grounded in the standards for which we are being held accountable, or if the decisions regarding the alignment of curriculum are not based on data about their students' achievement and learning needs. Only those closest to the students can make these decisions.

In one district that I work closely with, each elementary school is responsible for 2,500 standards, with each teacher within that school responsible for around 800 standards. To complicate matters, this district has dissected and made several standards from each original. That would be acceptable if the underlying meaning of the standards were kept intact, but several different teachers interpreted each standard differently, resulting in teachers and students who were confused and missed the mark.

We must provide teachers with a commonsense approach to examining and taming the standards by intentionally placing standards where there is a natural fit in the context of student learning and curriculum.

Packaging Standards into Grade Levels and Specific Classes

Some states package their standards by grade-level spans. For example, a set of standards might be mandated for kindergarten through third grade, but the standards might only be assessed in third grade. This design taps the experience of teachers to collaboratively decide at what grade level, how often, and at what level (depth and breadth) the standards will be addressed. Conversely, there are states that have already divided or grouped their standards by grade levels and in secondary schools by specific classes such as English I and English II.

Standards are organized in a variety of formats. Texas and California are among the many states that place their standards into grade-level packages prior to giving them to districts. A second-grade teacher can download the second-grade content standards from the state department of education website and begin examining the standards immediately. However, other states package their standards in spans of grade levels. For example, in

Massachusetts, standards are usually grouped into multiple grade-level packages such as math standards for grades one and two or science standards for grades seven and eight. When standards come in a grade span, teachers must make decisions about which year each standard is introduced, reinforced, and mastered. Teachers must decide collaboratively how to divide standards into grade-level packages that are developmentally appropriate for students and determine when, how, at what level, and how often each standard will be addressed.

Frequently, high school standards are in need of packaging also. At a curriculum meeting for a large high school, teachers were asked to align their standards and place them in the appropriate subject area classes where they would be addressed. After a few hours, a science teacher reported that many of the science content standards that spanned high school were not being addressed. He, like his colleagues in the science department, thought that all standards were accounted for through other classes.

During the packaging process for high school standards, teachers decide how often to include a standard and in which classes they need to be included (e.g., which standards will we address in Algebra I, how many of those will be repeated in Algebra II, and are there any remaining that were not addressed?). The point of creating grade-level packages or standards packaged by specific classes is to eliminate the possibility that any standard is omitted and to ensure that intentional repetitions are in place within those packages of standards.

If you teach in a state that does not provide grade-level or class packages of standards, teachers can collaboratively create them. Without these packages, teachers often omit or unintentionally repeat standards wasting valuable time that students could be using to delve deeper into the content.

Collaboratively Making Decisions About the Placement of Standards

A collaborative team familiar with the grade or content standards begins by selecting the standards that are essential at each grade level or in specific classes for students to know and be able to do. In some districts, districtwide teams are formed from experienced teachers who are selected to represent each content area. They work together to scaffold the standards from one grade to the next in each subject area. The team decides at what grade level or in which class each standard will be taught and at what level of difficulty. For example, one district brought together a large group of experienced teachers representing every content area and every grade level from kindergarten through twelfth grade. This district team was divided into smaller teams that were responsible for spiraling and creating grade-level packages and specific class packages for one content area such as science from kindergarten through twelfth grade. At least one teacher from each grade level was included on each team to provide insight into what was developmentally appropriate at a given grade level. Teachers represented secondary schools from all of the specific classes. The committees were able to vertically align curriculum, scaffold it from one grade level to the next, and increase or decrease the depth or breadth of the curriculum through a spiraling process.

By determining what is imperative, a team can design a plan to address the essential curriculum. While developing these grade-level or specific class packages of standards, teachers use their professional judgment to determine what is developmentally appropriate and to scaffold the standards to meet the developmental needs of a particular grade level of students. Once these grade-level packages of standards have been identified, the collaborative team is poised to identify umbrella concepts.

Integrating Curriculum Through Multiple Venues

Connections across content areas and into the real world provide opportunities for learning to be integrated for students in a meaningful way. Often teachers consider integrated curriculum to be simply singing a song in music class about the Revolutionary War, which is being studied in social studies. Although this is a form of integration, there are richer lines that can be crossed to facilitate connections. For example, by studying the purpose of the music, students will uncover emotions and learn of the hardships experienced during the time of the Revolutionary War. Integration should also cut into real-life application whenever possible to make learning more relevant. The following are some examples of learning that cut through a content area into application.

- Light spectrum and paintings
- Energy and industrialization, machinery, heat
- Geometry and construction, quilting, designing

It is obvious that when learning crosses content areas, it can become more meaningful to students. There are even more ways to integrate than those we have discussed. Another way to tie all content areas together is through *central integration.* By identifying the commonalities between content area standards, teachers can nudge students to explore the standards through a shared concept. This provides a filter to sift out connections such as what science has in common with math and social studies while teaching students about significant concepts that are the same yesterday, today, and tomorrow. The important concepts taken from and beyond our standards serve as a shared vision for all content areas and are called umbrella concepts.

Identifying Umbrella Concepts

If you could only pick one thing to teach your students during a unit of study, what would that be? If we give thoughtful consideration to that question, we realize that it would have to be a concept that is large enough to umbrella over lots of other concepts. We might teach a concept like *erosion* since through that concept students could learn about the Grand Canyon, soil, rocks, weathering, and expanding ice. We would select *erosion* because we would not want to limit their learning to just weathering. Indeed, if we chose one thing, we want it to be a big one. Now enlarge that vision and think of a concept even broader than erosion—such as *change*. If students studied through the concept of *change*, we could embed erosion, expanding ice, technology, resistant diseases, exploration, rational numbers, variables, reflective writing, immigration, as well as all of the concepts around erosion plus much, much more. Transfer that to the classroom and imagine the possibilities if we allow students to examine and explore their world through these broad concepts.

Although most teachers would agree in theory that this sounds good, they might argue that they are bound by their state assessments to stick to the standards. In this chapter, we examine standards to find those broad concepts that make better use of our students' time by allowing students to study multiple content areas through them. You will see that sometimes the broad concept is sitting right in the standard, and sometimes you must go beyond it to find a deeper meaning.

These broad concepts are *umbrella concepts*, and they are broad conceptual ideas that are embedded within and beyond the standards. They are abstract and function just as the name implies—they umbrella over *all* content areas. They are huge, big concepts that emerge from all content areas and from all facets of life. Umbrella concepts are gradeless, timeless, and durable. Students in the first grade are able to learn about the same umbrella concept as high schools students. Figure 1–1 is a list of umbrella concepts frequently found in state and national standards.

```
systems
relationships
change
patterns
elements
independence
dependence
processes
structure
order
connections
cycles
discoveries
```

FIGURE 1–1. Umbrella Concepts

Because none of the umbrella concepts in Figure 1–1 is content specific, each is broad enough to become a connecting vehicle for all content areas. To qualify, concepts should be capable of spanning all content areas and providing a common thread, a common focus, and a common vocabulary to what is being learned. All learning should connect to this conceptual umbrella so that it functions as an intellectual transportation system allowing students to transfer conceptual understandings from one subject area to another.

Consider the umbrella concept of *systems*. Primary students might learn about simple machines while graduate students may study systems within advanced technology. Both groups of students study some form of a system, but the topics have changed as learning is scaffolded. What umbrella concepts can you identify from the standards in Figure 1–2? The most frequently stated umbrella concept in Figure 1–2 is the concept of *systems*; however, other possible umbrella concepts that we identified from within and beyond our standards are also italicized.

All of the italicized umbrella concepts in Figure 1–2 are explicitly stated. When an umbrella concept is not stated, it is implied. It is easy to identify the stated umbrella concepts such as *systems* in Figure 1–2. What most of us miss is that another umbrella concept, *relationships*, is implied within the first social studies standard in Figure 1–2. It is important that we use common sense and professional knowledge of students' needs to look beyond our standards for an implied, deeper meaning.

Subject	Standard
Mathematics	1. Identifies *change* units within a *system* (measurement)
	2. Graphs points on a positive coordinate *system* (geometry)
Science	1. Knows the location of the planets in our solar *system*, their *relationship* to the sun that includes orbits, climate, their characteristics including moons, and that Earth is a part of this *interrelated system*
	2. Articulates the *relationship* between *structure* and function of cells
	3. Comprehends what an eco*system* is and is able to compare and contrast eco*systems*, describe an eco*system* including populations, individuals, animals, plants, and their *relationship* to each other
Social studies	1. Explains how economic *systems* encompass production, distribution, and the consumption of goods and services, as well as wants and needs
	2. Explains that the barter *system* is often for the benefit of people both economically and due to available resources

FIGURE 1–2. Sample Content Standards

To maximize student learning, it is important to begin by identifying the umbrella concepts embedded within and beyond each content standard. Again, these umbrella concepts should be broad enough to cross all content areas. Studying the standards will provide teachers with the opportunity to identify the umbrella concepts that answer the question, What is so important about this standard that students must know, understand, and be able to apply when they leave this class?

Another important step is identifying more than one umbrella concept within each standard as was illustrated by social studies standard 1 in Figure 1–2. Most standards have more than one stated or implied umbrella concept, and all need to be identified during this initial step of examining standards. Thus, the next step in this process, after identifying the grade-level packages of standards, is to identify all stated and implied umbrella concepts from every standard.

Content-Specific Concepts

Also embedded within each standard are concepts that are much narrower. These are *content-specific concepts* and they provide limited connectivity to other content areas. To better differentiate umbrella concepts from content-specific concepts, which only cross one or two content lines, examine the umbrella concepts in Figure 1–1 again. Notice that when you think of each of these concepts, no specific content area comes to mind.

Let's examine content-specific concepts more closely. In social studies standard 1 in Figure 1–2, the concepts of *production*, *distribution*, and *consumption* bring to mind social studies, even before we look at the chart. Designing a unit that integrates music and science into social studies (without forcing them to fit) would be difficult if we were trying to use the content-specific concepts of *production*, *distribution*, and *consumption* as the connecting thread. There is no natural connectivity available to every content area if integration is wrapped around concepts that are specific to only one or two content areas. Think of the concepts *force* and *energy*. What specific subject do these concepts bring to mind? These concepts are usually specific to science. On the other hand, think of *systems*. All content areas can fit under that umbrella concept if you think of living systems, number systems, solar systems, and government systems, just to name a few.

If you choose to design a unit around just one or two content areas, the use of narrower concepts may be justified. An example of using content-specific concepts might be a unit that is designed around two subject areas in which the content-specific concept is important. The concept of *symmetry* would be ideal to act as an umbrella concept in a math, art, and science unit, but it would find an unnatural home in social studies.

Figure 1–3 provides examples of content-specific concepts. Remember, these are concepts that usually bring to mind just one or two content areas. These concepts do not meet the requirements of an umbrella concept when integrating all content areas.

Content-Specific Concepts	Brings to Mind
democracy	social studies
justice	social studies
matter	science
economics	social studies, mathematics
measure	mathematics, music
liberty	social studies
exploration	social studies, science
evolution	science
survival	social studies, science
equation	mathematics, science
symmetry	mathematics, science, art
energy	science, physical education
force	science, physical education
algebra	math
geometry	math, visual arts
number systems	math
heat	science
rights and responsibilities	social studies
rhythm	music
audience	language arts
customs	social studies
institutions	social studies
scale	math, art

FIGURE 1–3. Content-Specific Concepts

Figure 1–4 illustrates how umbrella concepts can literally umbrella over many different content-specific concepts. For example, the umbrella concept *change* acts as an umbrella over all content areas. The arrows point to the content-specific concepts that will be studied under the umbrella of *change*. Thus, *change* connects all content areas together and provides a thread of connectivity. Without the umbrella concept, it would be difficult to make connections between these content areas.

Figure 1–5 is a worksheet that was used by teachers examining their social studies standards. Each umbrella concept found in the standards is listed. Tally marks are placed beside each as it reappears in other standards. By viewing the umbrella concepts from this perspective, teachers can easily

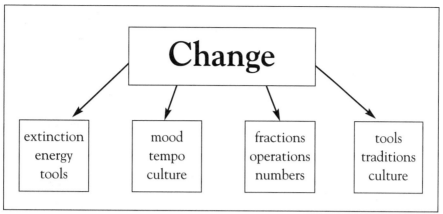

FIGURE 1–4. Umbrella and Content-Specific Concepts

see the umbrella concepts that emerge from the standards. Moreover, tally marks illustrate how many times each umbrella concept was found within or beyond the standards. The umbrella concepts *patterns*, *elements*, *systems*, and *process* emerge most frequently within the examined standards.

Only umbrella concepts from social studies standards are examined in

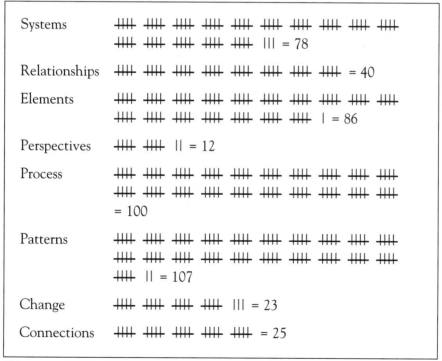

FIGURE 1–5. Social Studies Umbrella Concepts Identified from Standards

Social Studies	Science	Math	Practical Living
Systems (78)	Cycles	**Patterns** (68)	Movement
Relationships (39)	**Process** (61)	*Procedures* (20)	**Patterns** (42)
Choices	*Patterns* (55)	*Connections*	**Elements** (38)
Change (23)	Forces	**Systems** (52)	**Systems** (34)
Innovation	*Interaction* (9)	Operations	Functions
Strategies	*Discoveries* (9)	Reasoning	Procedures
Elements (86)	Functions	Symmetry	*Change* (21)
Perspectives (12)	Properties	**Processes** (56)	*Cause/effect*
Cause/effect	Communication	Properties	**Processes** (25)
Government	*Change* (4)	Concepts	Communication
Religion	**Systems** (48)	Movement	Principles
Institutions	Cells	*Change* (17)	Conflict
Culture	Tissue	Measurement	Behavior
Social	Organs	Principles	Fitness
Patterns (112)	Ecosystems	*Discovery* (2)	Balance
Customs	Energy	Ratio/proportion	*Discovery* (11)
Legacy	Environment	*Order* (14)	Physical wellness
Point of view	Organisms	Scale	Safety
Order	**Elements** (70)	Numbers	Lifestyle
Customs	Survival	Percents	Teamwork
Traditions	Extinction	Equations	*Order* (28)
Barter	Fossils	**Elements** (39)	Choices
Processes (100)	Adaptation	Formulas	Emotional and mental wellness

FIGURE 1–6. Concepts Worksheet

Figure 1–5. But, if all content areas are placed side by side, umbrella concepts that are the connecting threads are apparent. Figure 1–6 is a concept worksheet that includes four content areas. Most teachers find it necessary to list the umbrella concepts under each subject in this format because it allows them to easily identify umbrella concepts in all content areas. Content-specific concepts are also listed on this worksheet. The umbrella concepts that appeared most frequently and emerged as threads are in bold print. All other umbrella concepts are in italics while content-specific concepts are in regular font. By looking holistically at all content areas, teachers can find many different levels of connections.

Selecting Umbrella Concepts

We need things to make sense to us and to our students. Life is not divided into neat little compartments. It is important that students learn to transfer learning from one content area to another and into their daily lives. Learning that provides rich connections is easier to access and transfer outside of the school setting. Umbrella concepts should be broad enough to allow all subject areas to find natural connections. Thus, they become the most important thread of connectivity and help us achieve our goal: to develop rigorous and relevant curriculum that is easy for teachers to teach and natural for students to learn.

When examining standards, similar umbrella concepts often emerge. For example, we might find the umbrella concepts *properties* and *elements* within one standard. Both might be stated, or perhaps one is stated and one is implied. Since both are closely related in meaning, combining them under one of the two should be considered. We might eliminate *properties* and go with the umbrella of *elements*. Whether to combine both, eliminate one, or retain both will be decided after a close examination of the true nature and intent of what is within and beyond the standards. Before eliminating or combining, consider how the essence of the broad concept from the standards will be affected.

What happens when a standard does not seem to have an implied or stated umbrella concept? On occasion, we bump into a standard where the bigger idea is not initially apparent. If possible, go to the original source of the standard to determine the origin. Though rare, there may be standards that just do not seem to embrace an umbrella concept even when we look beyond them. Often standards that address discrete skills are the culprits. What happens to these standards? Miniunits or minilessons can be utilized to address these standards. It is important to keep an open mind, however. Frequently, during the teaching of a unit or lesson, new ways to integrate the standards, which initially appeared isolated or difficult to embed, can be found.

Look at the following sample list of standards. When the umbrella concept *relationships* is stated, it is bold while implied umbrella concepts are in parentheses.

- Writing: Write a narrative based on personal experience using well-organized ideas. (*relationships, order*)
- Writing: Write a narrative based on personal experiences using sensory details and descriptive language. (*relationships*)
- Writing: Write for a variety of audiences adjusting for style and content to each audience. (*relationships, connections*)
- Vocational Studies: Justify how work meets many needs for humans such as financial, emotional, and self-satisfaction. (*relationships*)
- Vocational Studies: Explain how the world has evolved and people have been able to settle in new places through the use of technology. (*relationships, change*)
- Social Studies: Understand the life of other cultures from their music, art, dance, language, artifacts, ceremonies, holidays, celebration, and institutions. (*relationships*)
- Social Studies: Justify how the human environment hinders or assists human activity and how the environment impacted where humans settled. (*relationships*)
- Science: Comprehend that internal cues affect individual organisms. (*relationships*)
- Science: Comprehend the **relationships** between structure and function of the parts of a cell. (*systems*)
- Mathematics: Understand how symmetrical lines relate to a variety of geometric shapes. (*relationships*)
- Mathematics: Compare and contrast two-dimensional shapes. (*relationships*)
- Mathematics: Apply the concept of equality. (*relationships*)
- Reading: Compare the **relationship** between a character's emotions and a character's behavior.
- Practical Living: Demonstrate cooperation with group members. (*relationships*)
- Practical Living: Demonstrates leadership and membership in a group. (*relationships*)

Notice that some of the standards imply the concept of *relationships* while other standards specifically state the concept within the standard.

Often, implied umbrella concepts are overlooked. This is why studying the standards is important.

While there is never a right or wrong umbrella concept, some appear better able to connect to other content areas. I have spent many hours debating the merits of whether a concept is broad enough or too broad to be effective. I have yet to find one within standards that is too broad. Very often standards are so broad that multiple umbrella concepts are present. Examine the following social studies standard:

> Understand the life of other cultures from their music, art, dance, language, artifacts, ceremonies, holidays, celebration, and institutions.

This standard could easily be repeated under the umbrella concepts *perspectives* and *connections*. In Chapter 4, we discuss how to narrow and focus student learning. But for now, identifying the umbrella concepts is not a step that can be omitted. Examining your standards is the only way that implied umbrella concepts will surface. Without the examination of standards, implied umbrella concepts embedded within and beyond the standards are often forgotten; therefore, opportunities for deeper understanding are missed. We must ask the question, What is so important about this standard that students cannot leave my class without knowing, understanding, and applying? Answer that question with common sense and professional knowledge, and the deeper meaning that underlies the standard will be discovered.

Language Arts and the Arts

As you have probably noticed, language arts and the arts are left out of most examples since we find that they are usually a beautiful fit with all content areas. Language arts typically have the standards strands of reading, writing, speaking, listening, viewing, language, and literature. The processes of reading, writing, speaking, listening, and viewing are the primary ways that students learn any content standard. A natural connection to all content areas exists inherently within these standards. Language usage and literature are appropriate connections for deepening knowledge and for students to demonstrate content learning.

As for the arts—visual and performing—many teachers have learned that using the arts as a way to connect to students' interest in an authentic way results in higher student achievement. Concepts in art are generally easy to connect to any content standard.

But We Already Teach Our Standards!

It seems so simple. If schools and teachers are held accountable for addressing standards, then all strategies and assessments should be aligned with standards purposefully to fulfill that mission. At an integrated curriculum workshop in a high school, a math teacher who was studying his standards found that he was spending one-half of his school year on content that either did not address the standards or just repeated the standards from the prerequisite class. While repetition is good, in this case, the math teacher saw no scaffolding or spiraling of standards. He wondered how he could take students to higher levels when the mandated standards were not being adequately monitored and addressed. Prior to this workshop, this teacher had believed that the appropriate standards were being addressed. Most teachers do not intentionally avoid addressing standards. Many teachers have never been invited to examine their standards in depth. Teachers want all students to achieve, but assistance, time, and training must be provided if teachers are expected to know the process for building a strong foundation.

Additionally, we bring to the table our own experiences and frames of reference. Collaboration with other teachers can provide an opportunity to examine standards closely and to consider perspectives and interpretations of each standard by other team members. Many teachers have not been provided with opportunities to challenge their own thinking; thus, student achievement eventually flatlines.

Pitfalls to Avoid

In addition to understanding their state standards, educators are also faced with the daunting task of selecting textbooks that align with the standards. Traditionally, textbooks have been the most used resource in schools. For years, they served as the only pathway for teachers to follow. Today, educators are realizing that a one-size-fits-all textbook does not allow all students equal access to learning. Textbooks provided teachers a map for teaching their content area and the added convenience of chapter tests and quizzes, which made teaching easier, but not better and in many cases, not even good. Research on how students learn has led teachers to question the blanket use of textbooks as the main resource. More and more teachers are beginning to value a classroom that is rich in print and other resources outside of textbooks.

Teacher Elisa Beth Brown stated, "As adults we rarely use textbooks for resources; instead, we use real-world resources. To provide our students with powerful, rich resources, we must model the use of resources such as trade and chapter books, reference materials, the Internet, journals, artifacts, experiments, interviews, newspapers, and other resources that are available." She recognizes that students need exposure to authentic resources and to more than one writer's point of view.

Virtually all schools and districts should examine evidence of student performance to assist in targeting areas of need. How could textbook authors possibly know that your class is full of students who are proficient in one area, yet in desperate need for more opportunities in another conceptual or skill area? In addition, we must meet the needs of the gifted students, and certainly we are recognizing our responsibility to provide and a student's right to expect an equitable education. Only teachers (and not textbooks) can answer the following questions:

- What concepts are embedded within this standard?
- How much time should be devoted to this standard?
- When should this standard be introduced?
- At what level should this standard be addressed?
- When will this standard be intentionally repeated?
- Can this standard be integrated with other content area standards?
- Is the scaffolding of standards included in our alignment?

Textbooks may very well be the most accessible resources we have, but they are just resources and should not serve as the conductor that orchestrates your students' instruction. Thankfully, many teachers are designing lessons grounded in the conceptual focus of the standards and the concepts within and based on evidence gathered from students' work. After working with state standards from across the country, I have concluded that lessons and unit designs must begin with standards, and that textbooks, as well as other resources, should be selected to support the curriculum. This is standards-based teaching.

Commercially Prepared Units
Just as textbooks do not hold the answer to teaching standards, neither do concepts or units designed by neighboring schools, districts, or states. Recently, twenty middle school teachers attended a workshop on curriculum standards. The out-of-state presenter provided the umbrella concepts instead of having teachers identify them from within or beyond their own standards. She informed the teachers which concepts would be good for framing a unit of study without ever asking teachers to examine their own state standards. Teachers were then given the task of plugging their stan-

dards into her umbrella concepts and designing lesson plans and units. Common sense tells us that we must begin with our own standards. This process resulted in teachers who had little ownership in the process and standards that, once again, are plugged into ready-made unit titles.

For years, educators have struggled to move away from the traditional approach of designing lessons and units first and then assigning standards almost as an afterthought. Teachers must examine their standards to determine for themselves which umbrella concepts are important. Approaching lesson planning by assigning arbitrary concepts and not retrieving the essence from your own standards is merely treading water. Looking within and beyond your standards must become the foundation for instruction, curriculum, and assessment designs.

Even if a presenter brings umbrella concepts that have been identified from your own state standards, chances are that the concepts will still miss the mark. Workshop facilitators do not know what your students have previously addressed, at what levels the standards have been addressed, and what the school's comprehensive plan has identified through school data analysis as areas for growth. Only practicing teachers have these answers for their school community. Experts can, however, bring an understanding of standards and a willingness to assist teachers in identifying their own conceptual unit framework from their own standards, based on their knowledge of their students. This process must include teacher discovery of the concepts embedded within and beyond the mandated standards. In fact, this process is as important as the product!

Standards-based planning should not be an artificial process. Umbrella concepts must be identified from within and beyond your standards, not standards from another state, textbooks, or from some expert's list of concepts. Since standards vary from state to state, from content area to content area within a state, and from grade level to grade level at each school, all schools must go through the process of alignment, lesson planning, and unit designing to avoid missing the opportunity to enrich standards that might otherwise be substandard. Regardless of whether we agree or not, we are employed to use the standards—so use them as a tool to go beyond and design a curriculum that is rich with opportunities for your students.

Ensuring Standards-Based Learning

As a principal, a teacher, or a district administrator, we are responsible for ensuring that all standards are being addressed and at high levels. Though this goal may sound reasonable, it can be an extremely frustrating and over-whelming task. Due to the pressures of this responsibility, I have observed principals become suspicious and even envious of other principals. They feel that the practices that lend to higher achievement, such as standards-based learning, are somehow being kept secret from them. I worked with a principal who actually thought that other schools and other principals had a secret that they were not sharing. Frankly, she was so sure that she was being left out of the loop that she once accused her husband, who was a principal of a high-performing school, of hoarding information from her so that her school would stay one step behind his.

The fact is that there is no secret. It is sadly true that there is very little information on the organization of standards. This lack of easy accessibility has left many educators floundering. While a few books have been published on what the end product should look like, few give the basic steps that lead to success.

One impediment to success is that there is little opportunity to learn from others who have put theory into practice. Teachers are inundated with three-ring binders full of resources, state standards, curriculum maps, units, lesson plans, national standards, alignment documents, and on and on. However, the one resource educators really need—more time—won't fit into a three-ring binder.

Given these problems, we need an approach to standards-based learning that eliminates the fluff and does not force teachers to spend hours of needless time getting ready to teach so they can spend more time teaching. When the standards are tamed, teachers will have unit frameworks that guide all lesson planning, thus allowing teachers to focus more on instruction and less on the alignment of standards.

Terms to Remember

Concepts: Big ideas that are universal, like *balance, change,* and so on.

Content-specific concepts: Broad concepts, like system of government, specific to the content standards.

Essential learnings: Things that the teachers determine are critical for their students to know and be able to do at each grade level. Also known as grade-level packages of standards.

Minilesson: Short lesson on essential learnings at the point of need; power lesson. May not fit under an umbrella concept.

Miniunit: Short unit on essential learnings at the point of need or a unit of short duration relative to a larger unit of study. It typically resides within a larger unit and is designed to scaffold learning.

Thread: A unifying idea that connects several content areas.

Umbrella concepts: Ideas like *change, relationships,* or *movement* that relate across curricular areas and have no specific content.

Further Reading

Erickson, H. L. 2001. *Stirring the Head, Heart, and Soul.* 2d ed. Thousand Oaks, CA: Corwin Press.

Fogarty, R. 1991. *Integrate the Curricula.* Palatine, IL: Skylight.

Marzano, R. J., and J. S. Kendall. 1996. *A Comprehensive Guide to Designing Standards-Based Districts, Schools, and Classrooms.* Alexandria, VA: Association for Supervision and Curriculum Development.

2
Bundling and
Cross-Bundling Standards

The process of bundling made me think about how I can rebundle in several different ways—it's the bundling and the planning to teach better through providing connections that makes this process a more powerful model. It is starting from scratch and not borrowing concepts and topics from here or there.

—Elisa Beth Brown, teacher, Auburn Elementary

When the standards movement was relatively new, several tools appeared on the market that were designed to assist teachers to identify which standards were addressed in each lesson. Do you remember the lesson plan books where teachers highlighted the standards they were addressing each week? There were several tools available as companies jumped rapidly into the fray to capitalize on the new interest in standards. Each school had its own method for keeping up with the standards.

The inherent problem with most methods was that standards were selected after the lesson had been designed. It was almost as an afterthought that I picked the standards that supported my lessons. Looking back on those days, it was obvious that I could make standards fit into any lesson—whether they did or not. On top of that, rarely was anyone held accountable to provide evidence of the congruency between the lesson and standards. It was more of a formality than a process.

As a principal, I rarely checked to see if there was a tight fit between the two when I reviewed lesson plans. Rather, I checked to see that teachers had identified the standards and almost any fit between the standards and the lesson would suffice. It is embarrassing to admit that I played that game also.

Textbooks drove our instruction and standards were matched to the lesson of the day. Today we know that to be most effective, lessons are designed around the standards and not the other way around. We know that standards drive our lesson designs, instruction, and assessment. If students are judged on the standards, then we teachers must provide them an opportunity to study what is within and beyond the standards and not just the next page in our textbook. The techniques presented in this chapter are designed to help you organize standards for student success.

Managing the Process of Bundling and Cross-Bundling

Early in my work with standards, I invited teachers to take a sheet of paper printed with the standards, and to cut the standards apart. Only one standard on each strip of paper. Teachers were then asked to place each standard in the pile under a previously identified umbrella concept that afforded a natural fit with each standard. Teachers were to *cluster* the standards by determining the best umbrella concept for each. Although the terminology and techniques have changed, clustering or bundling standards stays the same. Each standard is grouped under the umbrella concept that is embedded within and beyond the standard. No longer do teachers need to cut standards into individual pieces because a more efficient methodology for the process has been developed.

Finding a Natural Fit for Standards
Under the Umbrella Concepts

Bundling standards has been called *clustering, grouping, unraveling, aligning, unpacking,* and *repacking.* All of these terms mean one thing: to place standards under the umbrella concepts that provide a natural connection (stated or implied) to the standards. This raises the bar and propels students toward making connections to higher-order thinking and conceptual learning. Students can see that learning is not isolated. For example, students who discover that *patterns* are not isolated to one content area can use that same lens to investigate and predict population rates in a country for the next thirty years in social studies, solve problems by identifying patterns in math, use patterns to identify genes in the human body containing clues of future diseases, and identify a genre of writing in language arts. Students need to see that learning is not compartmentalized and that what they learn in one content area is applicable to others. Students are thus encouraged to make connections to concepts in other content areas and outside of school that have always existed, but that have not always been apparent.

    Cross-bundling is the intentional repetition of placing standards under the umbrella concepts so that standards will be purposefully repeated

Subject	Standard	Elements	Systems	Processes	Patterns
WR 1	Use the elements of writing in all content areas	✓			
WR 2	Use the writing process to write a narrative based on personal experience			✓	
MA 1	Create, recognize, extend, find, write, and apply rules for number patterns	✓		✓	✓
MA 2	Graph points on a grid		✓	✓	
SC 1	Identify the different layers of Earth and explain their composition	✓	✓		
SC 2	Comprehend the processes of construction and destruction that rocks perform		✓	✓	✓
SS 1	Examine basic components of the U.S. economic system	✓	✓	✓	
SS 2	Understand that government has problems of scarcity just like corporations and people		✓		✓
SS 3	Compare and contrast the United States, Canada, and Mexico		✓		✓

FIGURE 2–1. Bundling and Cross-Bundling Format

throughout the school year. If the umbrella concept *relationships* captures the essence of several standards, then all standards that fit under that umbrella concept would be marked, checked, or physically placed into the *relationships* stack. That is bundling. To cross-bundle, standards that need to be intentionally repeated will be placed under more than one umbrella concept. Since multiple umbrella concepts were identified previously, cross-bundling can now be easily accomplished.

There are many different ways to bundle and cross-bundle standards, but experience has taught us a methodology that is efficient and effective. Cutting standards into individual strips of paper is cumbersome and difficult. Figure 2–1 outlines a template that many teachers have found preferable. This format allows teachers to view standards holistically throughout the process of bundling and cross-bundling. This template was designed on a database in order to allow teachers to sort and re-sort standards when they had completed the bundling process. Standards in many states are available electronically and formatted so that they can easily be imported into an existing database, so there is no extra cost associated with technology. Several columns were added to the right of each standard in Figure 2–1. The previously selected umbrella concepts—*elements, systems, processes,* and *patterns*—determined the number of columns that were necessary. Only those umbrella concepts that encompass enough standards to justify a unit of study will be selected to umbrella a unit.

Figure 2–1 illustrates how standards can be flagged under one or more umbrella concept. Each umbrella concept will frame a unit. The number of standards identified in this process and the difficulty of each standard will determine the length of each unit. Using this form, teachers place a check mark (✔) in the appropriate box beside each standard each time it is included under an umbrella concept. When all the standards have been placed under the appropriate umbrella concepts, it is easy to see how often a standard has been intentionally repeated or if one has been omitted entirely. Occasionally, there may be a few remaining standards that initially did not seem to find a natural and snug fit to the umbrella concepts.

Figure 2–1 divides the school year into four different umbrella concepts. There are no hard-and-fast rules dictating the number of umbrella concepts that should be identified for use during a school year. Many educators who are on a school calendar divided into quarters favor the four-unit design simply because it provides closure to a unit prior to a break. Some teachers have designed six units of study based on their schedule.

However, a unit of study should not be developed based on any scheduling criteria; rather, umbrella concepts should be identified, and units should be developed based on the standards and the needs of the students. Even within one nine-week period, a teacher might include additional miniunits and minilessons because a few standards may not initially appear to find a natural home within a unit. Some teachers find that one umbrella concept works well for an entire year while others use the same umbrella concept for a semester or more. If the same umbrella concept is used to frame a unit longer than ten to twelve weeks, then usually this unit will have a different focus. For example, the focus might shift from relationships that are beneficial to relationships that are detrimental. This shift in focus will be explored more thoroughly in Chapter 4. Standards and students' needs dictate the length and focus of a unit.

Calculating When Enough Is Enough

The number of standards placed under one umbrella is important. After bundling and cross-bundling, teachers may find an overload of standards under one umbrella concept and perhaps not enough to justify a unit under another. If this happens, it may be better to extend the length of one unit and/or shorten the length of another. For example, if under the umbrella concept *connections* there were fifty standards and only twenty standards under *relationships*, then the unit on *connections* may last twice as long, or perhaps the standards under *relationships* could be reassigned to other umbrella concepts, eliminating that unit all together.

While it is important for standards to find a natural fit under an umbrella concept, that is not always possible. If a standard does not fit, skip it and come back to it later. Standards should not be forced under an umbrella concept. By the same token, if a standard naturally belongs to a group of standards, but does not seem to fit under the umbrella, it should still be bundled where the majority of that group of standards best fits. For example, if several standards about organisms fit tightly under the umbrella concept *systems*, but one of those standards seemed to lack a rich connection to *systems*, placing it with its group under *systems* will be the most natural fit. Pulling lone standards out of a cohesive group of standards will result in a jagged curriculum.

Though there is no precise rule for the number of standards that should be bundled under an umbrella concept, teachers frequently ask how many standards are too many. To assist teachers in determining a general rule, I examined multiple bundles to get an average number of standards that teachers were placing under each umbrella. Figure 2–2 outlines a formula developed based on the number of standards that experienced teachers have included in their bundles. These guidelines work best with math, science, practical living, vocational studies, and social studies. They may not work as well with reading, writing, and other disciplines that contain a lot of process skills. To find the number of standards that generally have been bundled under an umbrella concept, follow Steps 1 through 3 in the figure.

One of the main reasons we examine the number of standards that are in a bundle is to avoid the possibility of having lopsided bundles. By that I mean that if math has three standards in a bundle and science has forty, then it is obvious that the science portion of the unit will last much longer than the

Step 1	Step 2	Step 3
Divide the number of umbrella concepts into the total number of standards.	Divide the number from Step 1 in half.	Add the quotients from Steps 1 and 2 together to get the average number of standards to bundle and cross-bundle under one umbrella concept.
Example: 100 standards divided by 4 umbrella concepts equals 25 standards.	25 divided in half equals 12.5 extra standards.	Add 25 standards to 12.5 and there should be generally 37.5 standards per unit or umbrella concept (give or take 4 or 5).

FIGURE 2–2. Determining the Number of Standards in a Bundle

math portion. We found that to equalize our skeleton units across the entire year, we had to make sure that all content areas were relatively equal to each other. This provided a starting point to make further decisions about issues such as the approximate length of time that students will need to explore.

Repeating Standards Through Cross-Bundling

When standards are intentionally repeated within different units, cross-bundling has occurred. While standards are being examined and bundled, cross-bundling has to be done intentionally. Will every standard be repeated? Only teachers who know the importance of what is within and beyond each standard and their students' needs can determine this. However, keep in mind that students need repeated exposure to all concepts to achieve independence.

Beginning with Social Studies
Because social studies is naturally organized by the progression of time, this content area emerged as the logical beginning point for teachers who are

bundling standards. Science comes in neat packages such as life science and earth science, and math, although sequential, is still not as naturally sequential as is social studies. Language arts and the arts overlay all content areas beautifully so they are bundled last. Along with a logical starting point, the teacher or the collaborative team of teachers should have a copy of all the standards. Virtually all standards can be downloaded from each state department of education's website. Print out the standards and distribute them to all team members. They should read the standards one by one and discuss under which umbrella each standard should be placed, checking off each standard as illustrated in Figure 2–1.

By designing a template on a database, standards can easily be sorted, re-sorted, and printed. Usually some of these standards will change once the unit design or implementation is underway. Therefore, the use of a database template like Figure 2–1 is highly recommended as part of the bundling and cross-bundling process. A database template can usually be designed in a short period of time by a technology coordinator, and almost every district owns a database program. Separate fields should be designed to house standards, standard numbers (if standards are numbered, if not, number them), and grade level. In addition, add several columns, or fields as they are called in database programs, to the right of the standards so they can be checked off as they are designated to a specific umbrella concept.

The process of identifying umbrella concepts, bundling and cross-bundling standards takes time. Approximately one day should be set aside for this task. If there is any confusion, it usually lessens after bundling begins. It is not unusual for one to feel frustration in the early stages of identifying concepts and bundling standards. Even a veteran teacher can find this process daunting, as evidenced by National Board Certified teacher Belle Rush's reaction, "When we first began bundling our standards, I felt overwhelmed by the sheer multitude of the standards that we were expected to teach, especially since as a primary teacher I am responsible for all subjects. But, by carefully analyzing each standard it was clear that some patterns were emerging. Two umbrella concepts that were really repeated throughout were *relationships* and *systems*. These framed our entire year. By analyzing our standards, it was easier to see connections between content areas. Our next step was to put our standards into bundles that were connected, and then we had to decide when to teach each bundle. This process, although initially overwhelming, resulted in a clear direction for our school year that was full of connections that we would have otherwise never made."

It is to be expected that when teachers begin to implement their final units or sometimes as early as when they are using the standards to design the units, they will find better connections for some standards under a different umbrella concept. Teachers report that students frequently point out connections they have overlooked or not considered. Often teachers find that once teaching of the unit begins they need time to readjust their bundles and units. Thus, it is essential that follow-up for teachers be conducted regularly and frequently during the first year of implementation. Although collaborative meetings will always be needed to support standards-based integration, less time will have to be devoted to readjustments once the process is mastered.

But I Already Know My Standards
Teachers should expect some initial confusion, frustration, and long-term professional growth because that is what this process delivers. I remember well the frustration of teachers at a small elementary school who began to bundle standards while participating in an integration workshop. During the morning of the first day, a second-grade teacher continually rolled her eyes and made comments that she knew her standards well, and that she did not need to bundle and cross-bundle what she was currently teaching. Right before lunch another teacher asked her what she thought of placing a certain standard under the umbrella concept of *change*. The frustrated teacher stated that she had always taught that particular standard when she got to it in the textbook. Since the teacher did not remember that standard, she innocently asked the frustrated teacher if she would mind getting her textbook and finding the standard. When lunch came, everyone left except for the frustrated teacher. She spent her entire lunch hour attempting to locate that standard in her textbook. When everyone returned from lunch, she sat in tears. She confessed, "This standard is not in my textbook so I have not been teaching it. I had no idea that my textbooks were not addressing all the standards that my students are accountable to learn."

In another school, teachers made the same kind of discovery. They had been using six science kits to teach science the entire year. About halfway through the bundling process, all teachers on the team made the same realization: four of the six science kits were not addressing their state standards. These teachers found that they were letting a resource drive instruction rather than what was within and beyond their standards.

At the end of every workshop, there are always several teachers excited at how much they learned about their own standards. Lana Whitaker, also a National Board Certified teacher, noted, "Prior to the bundling process, our standards were like a jigsaw puzzle with many pieces missing or out of place. Our team came together and started reviewing the standards and looking for connections. Once the connections were made, the pieces of the puzzle started to form a picture. It was then that I was able to visualize the year's progression." Notice that this is not about how much the facilitators have taught them; rather, it is about teachers discovering, uncovering, and making connections for themselves, as we desire our students to do. Every school must consider both the vertical and horizontal alignment issues through a continual collaborative team effort.

Vertical Alignment

Vertical alignment of standards (grade-level packages) means to intentionally place standards at the developmentally appropriate grade level where the standards will be addressed. Standards can be packaged by individual grade levels such as standards for grade one, or they can be packaged for multiaged groupings of students such as a package of standards for grades one and two. The configuration of the packages depends on how students are grouped within a school. This provides a guarantee of two things.

1. Students are guaranteed the opportunity to learn a given concept, content, or process when appropriate.
2. Students will have background knowledge to scaffold to the next year's learning at an efficient pace.

Vertical alignment is the process of identifying the essential learnings that will create grade-level packages of standards. This step is completed prior to beginning the process outlined in this book. For example, perhaps standard Y is introduced and repeated in the first grade. The second-grade teachers need to know where students are on the learning continuum with standard Y. The second-grade teachers would not waste the students' time reintroducing standard Y; rather, they would scaffold on standard Y and take students to a deeper level of learning.

Vertical alignment ensures that essential learnings will not be omitted because a certain teacher does not favor teaching a concept or does not get to it during a given year, thus putting the students at a disadvantage the next year. Usually, a collaborative school or district team of teachers creates curriculum that is vertically aligned.

Horizontal Alignment

On the other hand, horizontally aligning standards means to intentionally place standards in a sequence that is appropriate for students in a given grade level. Horizontal alignment

1. ensures consistency in the content of a course, and
2. provides for ease of integration across course content and among teachers.

In other words, all third-grade teachers will follow a pathway that addresses the same standards. Sometimes there are reasons for students to transfer from one classroom into another during the school year. If the students in classroom X have finished the study of standards one through ten and the student who is transferring into that classroom has not had the same opportunity, then this student would immediately be at a disadvantage. However, if the curriculum were horizontally aligned, all teachers would be working under the same umbrella concept and addressing the standards within that bundle. Every teacher would not necessarily be teaching the same content every day, but all teachers would share the same pathway toward mutually agreed upon student learning goals. It is important to recognize that teachers within a grade level who plan together will still have students with very different needs. Therefore, planning to differentiate instruction to address those needs will prevent teachers from simply developing one lesson plan with the same activities and sharing it horizontally. Collaborative planning is important because together teachers can accomplish and learn so much more, but with every collaborative plan that you choose to develop, remember your students' needs are very real and very different from another teacher's. We must plan to meet the needs of the students by creating plans that address those individual needs.

Horizontal alignment is critical in providing equal access for all students to a learning experience of high quality from pre-kindergarten through twelfth grade. It ensures that the alignment is the same, no matter who teaches it. Algebra I is Algebra I regardless of whose class it is taken in. Scaffolding curriculum and addressing standards at a deeper level with each repetition during the school year is the essence of intentionally articulating an aligned horizontal curriculum.

Another advantage of vertical and horizontal alignment is the ability to align materials. Some schools may plan for instruction around available resources. For example, if a grade level has enough materials for only one class at a time to study in the lab, that grade level of teachers may configure their unit so that each class will need the resources at a different time during the implementation of the unit. Thus, teachers may be able to arrange the order of standards under an umbrella concept to accommodate needed resources. All standards will be addressed within a specified time frame, but Mr. Bain might use the grow lab at the beginning of the unit while Ms. Pate might address the standards on plant growth later in the unit when the grow lab is available.

It is important to remember that resources need to be vertically as well as horizontally aligned. Several years ago, an elementary school created a list of books that would be used at each grade level. This was to prevent teachers from using the same book year after year to teach a concept or skill. The principal in this school said that the list was created and distributed to all the faculty members. She said that less than two months later she found the second-, third-, and fourth-grade teachers all reading the same book that was listed on the book list as a second-grade book. It seems that teachers have their favorites too. In fact, some act as magnets and follow students from one grade level to another. Teachers who loop would not use the same book each year to teach the same skill or content except on rare occasions. Instead, they would use other materials to scaffold student learning. Resource materials and books should be included in the vertical alignment so students are exposed to a multitude of resources and books.

One more valuable point to keep in mind is that teachers in a collaborative team might all be addressing order, but because students are different, actual instructional designs will vary according to the needs of students. All teachers will not necessarily approach the lesson design in the same way. Teachers design lessons based on students' needs, and every teacher will infuse his or her own personality and style of instruction. It is important for teachers to collaborate on lesson plans, but it is equally important that teachers be allowed to bring their strengths in teaching to the students. However, all instruction should be designed based on proven and promising research-based practices with the identified needs of students driving the instruction.

What If I Am Not Part of a Collaborative Team?
Although collaborative teams working together to integrate are ideal, there are many schools that may not have the desire, funding, or the teacher allocation to make this a possibility. However, the bundling process can also work well for a teacher working alone. A teacher can bundle and cross-bundle by using the standards from one content area or by integrating standards from other disciplines.

Many successful teachers and schools began this way. Teachers who teach in a self-contained classroom are better equipped to see a big picture of all content areas and to make connections throughout their day. Many of the important learnings around this process were discovered through my work with middle and secondary teachers. Teachers at these levels were forced to create ways of making rich connections while keeping the process logistically possible. Teachers' learning seems more apparent for upper-level teachers simply because the communication gap between the content areas is usually wider in intermediate through high school due to the different organizational patterns such as departmentalization. Crossing disciplines and making meaningful connections to timeless concepts should be the ultimate goal; however, many teachers began as lone pioneers.

Help Wanted: Practitioners Needed!
Teachers are the most important ingredient in this process. Only teachers know how frequently standards should be repeated and whether those standards need a surface skimming or a deep dive into the pool of learning. Concepts are timeless, but the decisions on how to present the concepts are made with each new population of students. Teachers must use their professional judgment and their vast experience to guide this process. Principals, administrators, and other nonteaching educators cannot infuse the same quality into this process as can the ones who know students best— practicing teachers!

Pitfalls to Avoid

Early in our experiences of working with schools in developing a strong curriculum foundation, we found that technology needed to be used wisely in this process. One school used a word processing program only to find that standards could not be manipulated without cutting and pasting. It is recommend that a database program be used for this process. Although a spreadsheet program has been utilized in many schools, sorting and re-sorting is just easier to manage in a database. Most school districts already own a database, and with a just a little instruction, the benefits will outweigh any time invested in learning the program. Moreover, there are software packages that are designed to house, sort, and track standards once the bundling and cross-bundling is complete, as well as allow lessons to be built around the bundled and cross-bundled standards. Carefully study all programs before investing to ensure that the one chosen meets the needs of the teachers and benefits the students.

How Can This Process Impact Student Achievement?

Adairville Elementary School, a preschool through eighth grade center in Adairville, Kentucky, certainly has a great deal going for it. The school was named a National Blue Ribbon School in 2001, received the School Leadership Award in 1999 from the Philip J. Morris Company and the Collaborative for Teaching and Learning, was nominated as a National Middle School to Watch a couple of years ago, and has earned many other awards proudly displayed in the lobby and hallways. Teachers at Adairville began working on curriculum alignment over seven years ago. After seven years of successful and not so successful attempts at aligning curriculum and resources, the school has seen a steady climb in test scores.

Several factors contributed to the higher test scores; however, one key factor was that every year the majority of teachers at Adairville School frequently and systematically revisited integration and alignment. Needless to say, other schools are now working on integrated, standards-based curriculum alignment. Additionally, teachers from this district are being employed to assist other districts and schools in making the best use of their standards. Adairville students' test scores have brought national attention to a previously unknown school.

Summing Up

Bundling and cross-bundling is not a new process, but the necessary steps of the process have not always been easily accessible. My colleagues and I have worked with thousands of teachers during their journey to bundle standards. Teachers have worked endless hours only to throw out their first attempts. One school threw out eight days of work only to begin again. I have seen many teachers grow and am sure that the frustration you may experience will soon be replaced with pride and enthusiasm as students begin making connections.

The end goal is improved student learning. Through bundling and cross-bundling standards, building on vertical and horizontal alignment, a curriculum system for a classroom or a school will be developed that is both efficient and effective in delivering results in student learning.

Terms to Remember

Bundling: Placing standards under the umbrella concept that is implied or stated within the standards.

Cross-bundling: Intentional repetition of placing standards under the umbrella concepts where standards will be purposefully repeated throughout the school year.

Horizontal Alignment: Standards are aligned across the grade level so that there is consistency among teachers teaching the same content, and a communicated opportunity to connect across content areas.

Looping: Students stay with the same teacher for more than one year. The teacher moves with the students from one grade level to another.

Vertical Alignment: Standards are aligned from pre-kindergarten through twelfth grade to ensure an efficient curriculum system, and one that provides equal opportunity to learn at a high level. Through this process, essential learnings are identified as grade-level packages of standards.

Further Reading

Grant, J., B. Johnson, and I. Richardson. 1996. In *The Looping Handbook: Teachers and Students Progressing Together*, Aldene Fredenburg (ed.). Peterborough, NH: Crystal Springs.

Robb, L. 2000. *Redefining Staff Development: A Collaborative Model for Teachers and Administrators*. Portsmouth, NH: Heinemann.

Williams, R. D., and R. T. Taylor. 2003. *Leading with Character to Improve Student Achievement*. Chapel Hill, NC: Character Development.

3
Relating Topics to Standards

I knew we were making connections because my language arts students began saying that they were studying the same concepts in science that we were studying. At first my students thought that was an accident. It didn't take long for them to grasp that we were intentionally planning lessons that made connections. That was when it really clicked for me as a teacher!

—Kathy Dotson, middle school language arts teacher

Traditionally in education, we were taught to design units around topics. We taught units on plants, dinosaurs, leaves, and Pilgrims. We spent great quantities of time designing units and teaching about topics that the authors of textbooks deemed important. We also taught about topics that interested the students and us, too. In this chapter, we learn to identify and view topics through a different, more conceptual lens.

Make Learning Relevant

My mother used to say, "If you are worrying about something that in five years you will still be worrying about, then by all means, continue to worry. But, if you believe that in five years this particular worry will become insignificant, then stop worrying because it is not worth worrying about." What is important today may very well seem insignificant tomorrow, and the topics of today will be replaced by the important events of tomorrow. Such was the case on September 11, 2001. Many topics significant prior to that day now dim in comparison. Topics change as life changes, and as life changes, topics are reprioritized to determine what is and what is not significant and important for students to learn today. Topics can and will change. Conversely, concepts are constant.

Learning must be relevant and connect to the students in a meaningful way. Topics help make that possible. Let's examine two teachers within the same school district. Students in Miss Allen's class travel to the local river to study pollution, water cycle, living systems, and many other science concepts. Water samples are gathered and data is compiled to study when they return to school. Students in Mrs. Yell's class study the same concepts through a few experiments in their classroom based on the suggested topics from their science textbooks with water samples bought from the science supply store. Both teachers are providing some hands-on strategies, but only one is making available a personal and meaningful connection for the students. It is reasonable to assume that the students who study their own river are drawing conclusions and making predictions about their water supply. It is important to select meaningful and relevant topics so students can see the importance of their learning.

Topics

Topics are defined as smaller themes that are usually found within a content-specific concept. Often topics are nouns such as Early Americans, Lewis and Clark, *The Red Badge of Courage*, bears, and oceans. Many times we can wrap our hands around topics such as dinosaurs (not literally), but the content-specific concept of *extinction* is not tangible.

Topics are used to address concepts. For example, if *water cycle* is a content-specific concept, then possible topics used to teach that concept might be a pond, an ocean, or a lake. If it were possible to teach the water cycle without using topics as examples—which would not be a best practice—then *water cycle* could become the topic. For another example, if *cycle* is the umbrella concept and *water cycle* is the content-specific concept, then I could select from a multitude of topics. I might use a glass of water to demonstrate evaporation, or I might select a local river or a lake to explore. If all else failed, I would use a cup or a bucket of water. The important point is that as the teacher, I need the flexibility to make those decisions based on what is relevant, meaningful, and available to my students.

Uncovering the Topics

When we examined standards, we learned that umbrella and content-specific concepts were either stated or implied within each standard. The same is true of topics. The twist is that some topics will be completely absent from standards. Remember one of the standards that we examined in Chapter 1?

> Explain how economic systems encompass production, distribution, and the consumption of goods and services, as well as wants and needs.

In this standard, we have the stated umbrella concept *systems* and the stated content-specific concepts *economic, production, distribution, consumption, goods,* and *services.* There is no topic either stated or implied within this standard. It is absent. Another standard as simple as *understand barter systems* has no topic suggested within the standard either. Therefore, the teacher must decide what topic is best suited to explore the umbrella concept *systems* and the content-specific concept of a *barter system.* One teacher may use the trade between the Native Americans and early European settlers to address the concepts while another may use barter systems from different countries or from thousands of years ago. The constant is the umbrella concept of *systems* and the content-specific concept of *barter systems.* The topics to address these are not constant, but the concepts are.

So what criteria or considerations should a teacher have when considering topics that exemplify a concept that is incorporated into a standard? Actually, there are several considerations. Is this standard grouped with other standards that make reference to a specific topic, or is there a specific time period associated with this standard or group of standards? If so, then the obvious choice of topics would come from other standards or what was relevant at that time. If either of these gives you clues to the topic, then it would be an example of an implied topic.

Not only should we look for topics that may be present in similarly grouped standards, but also we should seize the opportunity to demonstrate that concepts used in different time periods and in different situations are still relevant and meaningful today. Through the use of multiple topics to address the concepts, fabulous authentic connections can be made. By comparing topics that are relevant today to topics that were relevant in the past, we illustrate to students that concepts are durable—again, topics are not. For example, I might ask the students, "When is the last time you traded something with a friend or family member?" The students then make a connection to their own lives.

There are many other possible resources for choosing topics. Some ideas are available on state departments of education websites or from released items from state and national assessments. Needless to say, the best resource for selecting topics to teach the concepts within and beyond the standards is the experienced teacher. Beginning teachers can lend a new and often innovative perspective in the selection process, but nothing beats the experience and insight that teachers, who are keenly aware of the developmental and learning needs of students and of their interests, can bring to the table. Additionally, experienced teachers are usually more familiar with the horizontal and vertical alignment of the curriculum standards including its scaffolding.

Topics are important for students to study and understand. They frequently provide a tangible lens through which students can study higher-level concepts. Your community's values and belief systems, your students' ages, your students' interests, and your talents will provide topics that can be used to teach concepts. In primary grades, students' families, your school, a local neighborhood, pollution in a local river, and their classmates may be the topics under the umbrella concept *relationships*. As a student matures academically and socially, the topics under *relationships* might shift from schools and neighborhoods to the relationships our country has with other countries, including trade agreements and treaties. It is significant to note that if relationships with other countries change, so might the topics. For instance, today it would be timely to focus on our country's relationship with the Middle East, whereas twenty years ago the Soviet Union might have been a timelier topic. Regardless of which relationship we study, the umbrella concept remains the same.

Topics of Significant Importance

There are topics that are of such importance and relevance to our students that we instinctively include them in our studies. We would not study living systems without including topics such as the *human heart, lungs,* and *blood vessels.* Therefore, these are topics that are of such importance that they do not have to be explicitly stated within our standards. We inherently know to use these topics even if the standard only says that students will study living systems. I would not study the circulatory system without using the topics of *arteries, veins,* and *capillaries.* Many topics are stated within standards because they are deemed topics of significant importance. For example, under the umbrella concept of *systems,* the standards might state that students are to explore the system of weather. It is obvious that under the content-specific concept of *weather* one of the topics must be the Earth. This is not only relevant, but it would be ridiculous to assume that the standard expected students to explore the weather system on a faraway planet. Therefore, one topic under *systems* has been predetermined by the implied topic embedded within the standards. This topic is of such importance that it cannot be replaced with other topics. Figure 3–1 shows examples of standards that have predetermined topics. These examples illustrate very explicit topics while other standards allow for a broader range to be explored.

Standards	Topics
The Constitution of the United States is a flexible document that changes (amendments) and is interpreted (judicial review) over time to meet the needs of its citizens.	U.S. Constitution Amendments Judicial review
The United States, Canada, and Mexico have basic similarities and differences such as immigrants, colonial backgrounds, and cultural characteristics.	United States Mexico Canada
Identify similarities and differences in musical elements used in the music of Native American, American Folk, and West African cultures.	Native American music American Folk music West African music
Students will be able to describe properties of, give examples of, and apply to real-world situations whole numbers from 0 to 100,000,000.	Whole numbers to 100,000,000

Core Content for Assessment, Version 3.0, September 1999. Kentucky Department of Education.

FIGURE 3–1. Standards with Stated Topics

Figure 3–1 gives evidence that if a unit is to be designed based on these standards, the U.S. Constitution and its amendments are topics that cannot be omitted and are predetermined by the state standards. Furthermore, the figure provides the topics for studying musical elements. The stated topics of Native American, American folk, and West African cultures leave little room for doubt about what to explore. We might have chosen to examine music from other countries to address the musical elements if the topics had not been explicitly stated within the standards.

On the flip side, there are many standards that allow teachers a choice in the topics they use to address the standards and the umbrella concept. Figure 3–2 illustrates examples of standards from which topics can be selected based on students' interests, groupings of standards, or from the teacher's professional judgment.

Standards	Possible Topics
All cultures develop institutions, customs, beliefs, and holidays reflecting their unique histories, situations, and perspectives	United States, Canada, Mexico, or France
Productivity can be improved by specialization, new knowledge, and technology/tools	Businesses such as agriculture, transportation, and/or the military
Identifying various purposes for creating works of art	The pyramids of Egypt, Statue of Liberty, or Van Gogh

Core Content for Assessment, Version 3.0, September 1999. Kentucky Department of Education.

FIGURE 3–2. Standards Without Explicitly Stated Topics

Standards Vary in Form and Format

The process of identifying concepts and topics is more difficult because there is not a consistent format for standards in this country. Some state standards read more like a list of objectives while other states may have standards that are broad and conceptual. Even standards within a state may vary in form and format from content area to content area and span the spectrum from skill-like standards to higher-level standards rich with concepts. Some standards are written conceptually while others are written as if to micromanage the curriculum. Just when you are getting the hang of identifying concepts and topics in your standards, you might find that the style and format of your standards change when you go from one content area to another. Do not let this confuse you. All standards ultimately have concepts and topics either stated, implied, or absent. Remember, part of this process is seeing beyond the standards. If the standards in your state are not up to par, then you have a responsibility to reach beyond and find the topics and concepts that bring them to life. You might revisit the place of origin of a standard, or better yet, uncover new and interesting topics that will reach out and grab your students' interest.

Okay, I Am Still Confused!

After many years I still find myself confused every now and then. This is normal and part of the process of learning. Many teachers ask whether something is a topic or concept. It is sometimes difficult to make a distinction between the two. At times, we all find ourselves saying, "If this were used one way, could it be a concept and if it were used another way, could it be a topic?" The bottom line is that the final decision will ultimately depend on what the essence of each standard is and what topics or concepts will best allow students to explore, discover, and uncover the higher meaning within and beyond the standard. Keep in mind:

- If it is tangible, it is rarely a concept.
- Concepts are the same for first graders as they are for college students. The topics used to teach the concepts might change, but the meaning of the concept remains the same.
- Topics can, will, and should change as the world evolves and as new events occur, new discoveries are made, and as teachable moments appear.

Teachable Moment?

Recently, a national speaker at a leadership conference told this story, which I have paraphrased.

> A teacher asked me what had happened to those teachable moments such as when a bird flies in the window of a classroom? I told her that today you stop, examine the bird, discuss the bird, and research the bird, but tomorrow you are to close the window in your classroom.

That spoke volumes about her interpretation of standards-based education and the typical view that standards-based education has made teachable moments obsolete. Was the bird flying into the classroom a teachable moment? Only the teacher knows the answer to that question. What is apparent, however, is that if we teach by using topics to organize our instruction, we limit new information such as current events, teachable moments, and new discoveries. Conceptual teaching is much less restrictive because concepts are by definition broader than topics.

When the bird flew into the classroom, I would be hard-pressed to make a case for using that teachable moment in the middle of a unit on rocks. But, what if I were organizing a lesson around the umbrella concept of cycles? It might then be possible that an umbrella concept would provide connections that did not shift the focus of our unit. Students could examine birds in the context of migration, life cycles, or even discuss the cycles by which birds are affected. Since you know that the concepts within and beyond your standards guide instruction, it would be absurd to miss an opportunity to engage students through the identified conceptual filter if relevant connections were beneficial to their learning.

Teachable moments and topics of interest are important strategies used to motivate and pique the interest of students. Additionally, teachable moments are inquiry-based learning. With conceptual organization, often these moments can be utilized to teach to a higher level, to assist students to make sense of their learning, to make connections, and to transfer conceptual knowledge.

Pitfalls to Avoid

It is difficult to throw out a favorite unit or lesson. As Sylvia Abell, a writing consultant says, "It is even harder to throw something out if you have the poster that goes with the unit." Often when teachers are learning about this different way of looking at standards, they become frightened that this process will force them to toss out the units and lessons that they hold close to their hearts. Although there are instances where this will be necessary, it is not the norm. Many existing units and lessons fit snugly with conceptual learnings and mandated standards. Teachers frequently discover through this process that many units and lessons require only small refinements or adjustments to refocus students on the conceptual learning within the standards. We are possessive creatures by nature, which makes it difficult to give consideration to whether a topical unit or lesson needs to be eliminated. Enter into this process with an open mind. Make decisions based on what is embedded within and beyond the standards and what is best for students, not based on a favorite unit or the next chapter in a textbook.

During a work session on standards alignment, a primary teacher discovered that she was exploring topics that did not support the conceptual learning of her standards. She actually cried when she discovered her unit on dinosaurs did not address the essence of the conceptual learning within her standards. She explained that she had taught this unit for years, and the students loved it. She spent a long time perusing her standards searching for a fit that did not exist. The wonderful thing about this process is that no one told her it did not fit. She discovered it for herself. At the end of the work session, she approached a teacher who taught the next grade level and who would be teaching the concepts of *extinction* and *change over time*. Tearfully she handed over her unit. The teacher receiving the unit examined it carefully and informed her that she was already addressing these concepts using an almost identical unit. These two teachers, at different grade levels, had their students investigating extinction in almost identical ways. Needless to say, to expose students to a broader spectrum of learning, teachers need to be keenly aware of the importance of scaffolding learning and of examining standards.

Another memorable event was when a teacher discovered she was spending an entire semester teaching topics and concepts that did not support any of the concepts within or beyond her standards. She admitted that it would be hard to give up what she was accustomed to teaching, but she did not cry. With this discovery, she became excited because she now held the key for raising student achievement in her class.

One of the hardest lessons I learned while facilitating a workshop around bundling standards was to keep textbooks and other sequenced resources out of the room. A group of middle school teachers bundled their standards in record time using their textbooks and a resource manual—in about fifteen minutes when it normally takes several hours. I discussed this with the principal, who informed me that the teachers were in a bit of a hurry. I attempted to intervene to no avail. I have since watched this school's test scores steadily decline. Now, I have a rule: No textbooks or resource manuals are allowed until the process is complete!

For every teacher who finds that his or her standards are not being adequately addressed, there are many more who find only small chunks of learning that need to be refocused. This process should not elicit fear, but it should bring encouragement to know that we do not have to work harder, just smarter.

An Example from Middle School

Olmstead Middle School teachers use topics to address the bigger concepts within their standards. Figure 3–3 illustrates how topics are utilized to explore the loftier concepts. The topics in social studies were stated in the standards, but in the dance standards the topics were absent. The teachers made an intentional decision to use the topics from social studies—Festivals of Dionysus, Ancient Greece, Africa, Ancient Rome, and China—to explore different *systems* of dance. A topical connection between dance and social studies, as well as the conceptual connection through the umbrella concept *systems*, is the beginning to making connections. In this process, teachers are systematically articulating connections between content areas through umbrella concepts, content-specific concepts, and topics. When a connection cannot be identified, one should not be forced such as using George Washington's crossing of the Potomac River as a way to connect to the water

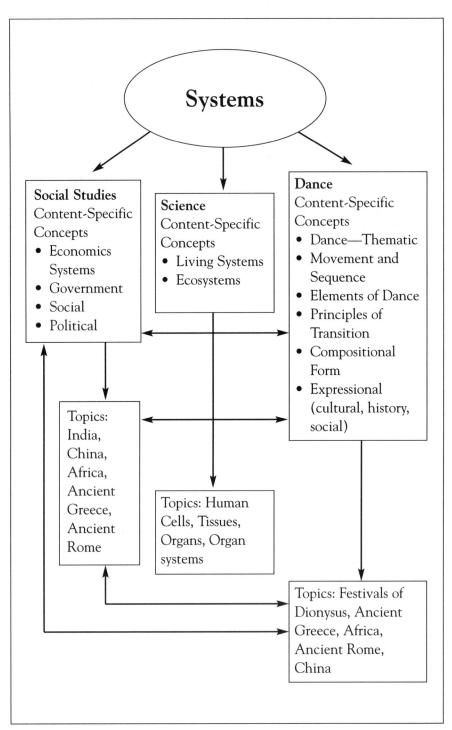

FIGURE 3–3. Middle School Worksheet

cycle or using the concept of beat in music to connect to a science lesson on the human heart.

Teachers and their students are discovering rich connections together. Olmstead Middle School teacher Susan Walker reports that she is amazed by the connections her students are pointing out to her.

Figure 3–3 is an actual working document. Although these teachers are just beginning this process, they are committed to improving student achievement through integration, by reaching within and beyond their standards, and by embedding research-based practices into their classrooms.

Sorting Standards

In Chapter 4, we will be designing questions based on the bundled and cross-bundled standards. To make this process flow more smoothly, it is a good idea to sort standards at this point. As soon as standards are bundled, and concepts and topics identified, they need to be sorted and packaged by the umbrella concepts. The use of technology such as a database makes this a very simple process, because standards can be sorted and re-sorted by bundles and removed or duplicated when necessary.

Experience has proven that sorting standards into the bundles by the umbrella concepts makes this process faster. The process of sorting should be completed immediately after all standards are assigned to an umbrella concept. By sorting standards into bundles, we can work with one bundle at a time, and place the others aside until we are ready to work with them. This is not a mandatory piece of the process, but it is suggested to make handling the bundles easier. However, if you don't have access to a database program, load your standards into a spreadsheet and cut and paste your standards into a bundle.

Study Figure 3–4 to see how our standards look prior to sorting them into bundles. Now, examine Figure 3–5 to see how a small bundle of standards will look after they are sorted by the umbrella concepts of *elements*, *systems*, *processes*, and *patterns*. Once all of the bundles are sorted, print and distribute them to the collaborative team.

In Figure 3–5, the umbrella concepts are sorted so that all standards are bundled under the umbrella concepts. The figure illustrates samples of the final products from four sorts. Each bundle is clustered together, which allows us to print each bundle individually.

Database programs have a function called *sort* that allow you to select the fields or items that you want grouped together. Select the field or column that houses the check marks made by the standards under one

Subject	Standard	Elements	Systems	Processes	Patterns
WR123	Use the elements of writing in all content areas	✓			
WR124	Use the writing process to write a narrative based on personal experience			✓	
MA111	Create, recognize, extend, find, write, and apply rules for number patterns	✓			✓
MA122	Graph points on a grid		✓	✓	
SC100	Identify the different layers of Earth and explain their composition	✓	✓		
SC101	Comprehend the processes of construction and destruction that rocks perform			✓	✓
SS188	Examine basic components of the U.S. economic system	✓	✓		
SS202	Understand that government has problems of scarcity just like corporations and people		✓		
SS303	Compare and contrast the United States, Canada, and Mexico				✓

FIGURE 3–4. Unsorted Bundled Standards

umbrella concept such as *elements* and click *sort*. This is relatively simple, but for more information on the process see your technology coordinator or refer to the software user's manual.

Don't get confused by the increase in the number of standards from Figure 3–4 to Figure 3–5. Standards were not added to this bundle; rather, the intentional repetitions of cross-bundling are now visible in Figure 3–5. The number of standards in these examples began with the nine original standards in Figure 3–4, but after the standards were bundled, cross-bundled, and sorted, the number of standards increased to fourteen due to intentional and purposeful repetition as illustrated in Figure 3–5. We are all aware that some standards need to be repeated in every unit we design to

Subject	Standard	Elements	Systems	Processes	Patterns
Elements					
WR123	Use the elements of writing in all content areas	✓			
MA111	Create, recognize, extend, find, write, and apply rules for number patterns	✓			✓
SC100	Identify the different layers of the Earth and explain their composition	✓	✓		
SS188	Examine basic components of the U.S. economic system	✓	✓		
Systems					
MA122	Graph points on a grid		✓	✓	
SS202	Understand that government has problems of scarcity just like corporations and people		✓		
SC100	Identify the different layers of Earth and explain their composition	✓	✓		
SS188	Examine basic components of the U.S. economic system	✓	✓		
Processes					
SC101	Comprehend the processes of construction and destruction that rocks perform			✓	✓
WR124	Use the writing process to write a narrative based on personal experience			✓	
MA122	Graph points on a grid		✓	✓	
Patterns					
SS303	Compare and contrast the United States, Canada, and Mexico				✓
SC101	Comprehend the processes of construction and destruction that rocks perform			✓	✓
MA111	Create, recognize, extend, find, write, and apply rules for number patterns	✓			✓

FIGURE 3–5. Re-sorted Bundled Standards for the Umbrella Concept of *Elements*

provide for mastery. This brief example illustrates that the number of standards will increase a great deal due to the cross-bundling process.

Final Thoughts

Because I have three children of different ages, a four-, twenty-, and twenty-five-year-old, I find myself having to learn what is important, significant, and relevant to each in order to have even a reasonably meaningful conversation with them. As each child matures, the topics that interest each changes. For example, my twenty-year-old son is for the first time interested in how his college transcript will follow him forever, my oldest daughter wants to know more about exterior color schemes for homes, and my four-year-old not only keeps me tired, but she wants to know why I think there is only one moon in the sky when she knows there are many because they all have different shapes, and all of my children want to know more about terrorism. I seize upon their interests and the topics of significant importance to gently help them to discover their answers. Teachers do the same thing by carefully selecting relevant topics of interest that foster natural inquiry.

Terms to Remember

Teachable Moment: An unexpected opportunity that occurs and that offers unique ways for students to discover new learning.

Topics: A smaller idea that is usually found within a content-specific concept.

Further Reading

Caine, R. N., and G. Caine. 1994. *Making Connections*. Parsippany, NJ: Dale Seymour.

Daniels H., M. Bizar, and S. Zemelman. 2001. *Rethinking High School: Best Practice in Teaching, Learning, and Leadership*. Portsmouth, NH: Heinemann.

National Research Council. 2002. *Helping Children Learn Mathematics*. Washington, DC: National Academy Press.

4
Refining the Concepts
Through Questions

*If we wish to evolve as educators, we must continue to question our-
selves, our methods, and the ever-changing world around us. To
enable the learners in our care, we should inspire them to ask and to
answer questions—questions that will make them want to open doors
and peek inside.*

—Susan Walker, Olmstead Middle School teacher

In the previous chapters, we examined standards to identify the umbrella
concepts, content-specific concepts, and topics, primarily because high-
stakes accountability insists that educators become fully cognizant of what
is important for students to know, do, and apply. By pulling the concepts
and topics from the standards, we discover what lies beneath the surface
and, in the process, begin to see the possibilities. Because a deep understanding of these possibilities promises to promote a higher level of student
achievement, which is the ultimate target, we take this process a step further and position the target so that students can focus directly on it.

Keep Your Eye on the Target

Without a deep examination of the standards and the understanding of
what is within and beyond the standards, it is easy to stray from the embedded conceptual learning. It is human nature to wander. Just think of a time
when you were a member of a group that was given a task to complete. Did
your group ever drift from the assignment to discuss your children, your
spouses, or the new table you wanted to purchase?

If adults frequently demonstrate off-task behavior and a lack of focus,
imagine a classroom filled with students. Think of an instance when your
entire class demonstrated off-task behavior. Maybe a student brought up a
point that you found interesting, and before you knew it, you were excited
and talking about something that piqued your interest. Eventually, you may

have heard yourself rambling and realized that you were not using the students' time wisely. We all know that a favorite student game is to get us off of the topic. Students are masters at manipulating the focus of the class—especially when they are neither engaged nor interested. So, how do we do both engage and interest students while keeping true to the standards? The secret is the art of questioning.

If Curiosity Doesn't Kill the Cat, Boredom Will

We have learned that umbrella concepts and content-specific concepts are the foundation, and that topics provide the concrete, tangible examples. Often, however, digressions occur because students aren't motivated to stay on task. But, what makes learning relevant and authentic? What makes students want to know? How can we pique the interest of students while maintaining the integrity of what lies beneath the standards?

As a mother of a four-year-old, I have been reawakened to the world of curiosity and wonder. My two oldest children are grown, and the memories of their nonstop questions have faded over the years. Now, I am experiencing déjà vu, and I frequently find myself exasperated by my daughter's incessant and excessive questions, even though I understand and appreciate their value and necessity. Young children are constantly asking a variety of questions, and she is no exception. I couldn't possibly remember all of her questions, but I could categorize them. Some questions were relevant to the context of her surroundings while others were based on her comfort and need. Maybe you will recognize a few of the comfort questions.

- Are we almost there?
- May I unbuckle my seat belt?
- How can I lie down with a seat belt on?
- Can you stop so I can go potty?

Other questions were constructed to expand her knowledge. These questions were formulated in and by the context of her surroundings—the backseat of a car with only her markers and a piece of paper.

- What color do red and blue make?
- Will you be mad if I get this marker on your seat?
- Will marker come off of my shoes?
- Does blue start with *b*?
- Does but(t) start with *b*?
- What does "since" mean?

You get the point. Children are born with a natural curiosity that is necessary to their learning. They naturally construct meaning through questions, inquiry, and experiences. Without this innate wonder, huge gaps would exist in their learning.

Albert Einstein believed that questions were important and that curiosity existed for a reason as evidenced by a life that was full of wonder. Questions are the articulation and vocalization of that wonder. They frame our problems, issues, and desires. Can you imagine the world without questions? Great inventors, scientists, mathematicians, researchers, and others had to initially frame their desire to know or their hypothesis by asking questions such as the following:

- Suppose . . . ?
- What if . . . ?
- What would happen if . . . ?
- How could one . . . ?

Ask a Boring Question, Get a Boring Answer
In G. Ivan Hannel's book *Highly Effective Questioning: Developing the Seven Steps to Critical Thinking*, he states, ". . . good and engaging . . . instruction through questioning is our best hope to unleash the learning potential of our students" (2001, 7). So how can we use our students' innate curiosity to enhance learning? In the classroom, questions are used to pique the interest of students as well as to provide a clearly articulated focus for the lesson. They inherently insinuate and conjure up the mysteries and emotions of investigation, problem solving, interrogation, inquiry, exploration, and research. Interesting questions motivate and hook students if they are developmentally appropriate, clear, and concise. The mysterious nature of questions will fizzle and die if the question is shrouded in too many words or in words that are not developmentally appropriate.

Questioning is not a new concept to any teacher. Teachers have traditionally and routinely used questions to assess their students' understanding, knowledge, and skill levels. These are important questions and should be designed to accompany instructional strategies. However, for the purposes of maintaining a focal point and engaging students, we discuss three types of questions in this chapter that are not specifically designed to assess the skill level or discrete content knowledge of students. Rather, we examine questions that are used to frame units, strategies, miniunits, or discussions and to pique the interest of students, to promote higher levels of thinking, to make learning relevant, and to maintain a clear, well-articulated focus for students and teachers.

Three types of questions anchor our standards-based units by wrapping around student expectations, concepts, skills, and topics:

1. Umbrella Questions
2. Essential Questions
3. Guiding Questions

As we begin to explore and construct our questions, let us agree to adhere to the following tenets:

Questions

- Should be open-ended as much as possible. That is, questions that have one right answer should offer students multiple avenues to arrive at that answer, or questions should have more than one right answer or no right answer.
- Should require more than a yes or no answer.
- Should promote a high level of thinking and not simply recall or list answers unless they are designed to assess specific skills or discrete content knowledge.
- Should challenge students and be thought-provoking.
- Should be framed from the students' perspective, if possible.
- Should be interesting and relevant to students.
- Should be accessible by all students and free of biases.
- Should be designed by or have student input, whenever appropriate or possible.
- Should be fine-tuned as we learn about our students' abilities.
- Should scaffold learning so each builds on new knowledge and allows students to apply knowledge in multiple situations.

Umbrella Questions

Umbrella questions, like umbrella concepts, are designed to cover an entire unit of study. As such, they become the binding thread between content areas. Umbrella questions connect students to the standards, promote high levels of thinking, assess student progress, maintain a focus, and ignite students' interest in relevant ways.

Focusing Is the First Step in Developing Umbrella Questions
Before developing umbrella questions, think about the broad and abstract umbrella concepts from Chapter 1. It is easy to flounder and lose focus dur-

ing a unit of study unless we take care to narrow and clearly define the focus. For example, the umbrella concept of change is so broad that if we were to brainstorm a list of "what change means," the following conceptual statements might emerge:

- Change is inevitable.
- Change is sometimes spurred by humans and at other times caused by natural events.
- Change may be positive.
- Change can occur gradually over time.
- Change can be sudden.
- Change can be permanent.
- Change can be temporary.
- Change may be necessary.
- Change may be halted.

When you consider the vast number of different interpretations each of us brings to the table for the umbrella concept of change, this list could be lengthy. Indeed, the lack of focus might take students and teachers in directions that are very different from the intent of the standards. And, what is the intent of the standards? There is no way of knowing which of these statements provides the best lens to discover the learning embedded within and beyond our standards unless we really understand our standards.

From Umbrella Concepts to Umbrella Questions

To make the process of developing questions less daunting, we begin by looking at our standards through the lens of the umbrella concept. We examine the standards and brainstorm a list of what the essence is that lies within and beyond the standards in conceptual terms. Begin the process by looking at one bundle of standards and the corresponding umbrella concept, and

1. List all of the possible attributes about the umbrella concept that are apparent in the standards.
2. Reexamine your bundle to see if some of the standards may fit more appropriately in another bundle, or perhaps you now see that a standard in another bundle could also be added to this bundle.
3. Survey your list of attributes and establish which one or ones best capture the essence of the majority of the standards within that bundle.
4. Write a statement or two that seizes the meaning of the bundled standards through the umbrella concept, and then articulate student expectations for these standards that are common and mutual

to all content areas. These mutual student expectations are called *mutual umbrella expectations*.

It is important for teachers to articulate their expectations for students. "I want my students to pass a final exam" is not an articulation of student expectations. In addition, each content area will have its own expectations for students that are specific to that subject. Student expectations, both mutual umbrella expectations and essential content expectations, are identified concurrent to the development of the questions. In this simultaneous process, alignment remains intact.

For the moment, we will discuss only mutual umbrella expectations and umbrella statements. Figure 4–1 provides a high school example of how a small bundle of standards and the umbrella concept can be transformed into an umbrella statement and mutual umbrella expectations. Three different subject areas are represented in this example.

Keeping these mutual umbrella expectations and statements in mind, compare them to the following umbrella questions. Consider if the correlation is visible. Make sure the questions are well articulated. Observe that both of the questions capture the essence of the mutual umbrella expectations and the umbrella statement. In addition, both questions use a pronoun such as *I* or *my* to connect the learning to the students' world.

Umbrella Questions (High School Unit: Patterns)
- How can I use patterns to solve problems and to make predictions?
- How do patterns create harmony in my life?

Now, let's return to the middle school example from Chapter 3. This brainstormed list of statements from the bundled standards in Figure 4–2 will build on the previous work from the Middle School Worksheet (page 44). In Figure 4–2, teachers have continued the process by developing umbrella statements using the attributes from their standards and their umbrella concept of systems.

The teachers discussed each of the standards within this bundle, as well as their interpretations of the umbrella concept. Once the standards were put on the table with the umbrella concept, the focus began to narrow. After much discussion and examination, the teachers decided that the following statement was the thread or umbrella statement that provided the best connection between content areas while honoring the essence of the standards:

Systems have parts that work together to perform a function.

Standards:

SS-H4.1.3 (Social Studies)
The location and distribution of human features on Earth's surface are based on reasoning and patterns.

SC-H-1.2.2 (Science)
An element is composed of a single type of atom. When elements are listed according to the number of protons, repeating patterns of physical and chemical properties identify families of elements with similar properties. The periodic table is a consequence of the repeating pattern of outermost electrons.

RD-H-3.0.13 (Reading)
Identify a variety of persuasive and propaganda techniques and explain how each is used.

Umbrella Concept: Patterns
Umbrella Statements
- Patterns help us make sense of the world.
- The world is very organized and through the use of patterns, many discoveries have been and can be made.

Mutual Umbrella Expectations: At the end of this unit, students will . . .
- Patterns provide logic to many aspects of the world.
- Identify patterns in the world.
- Use patterns to solve problems.
- Unravel patterns.
- Make predictions based on patterns.
- Compare and contrast a variety of patterns.
- Use evidence to support the statement: Patterns create harmony.

Core Content for Assessment, Version 3.0, September 1999. Kentucky Department of Education.

FIGURE 4–1. From Standards to Mutual Umbrella Expectations

Along with this statement, the following mutual umbrella expectations were identified.

- Different parts of a system perform different functions.
- Systems are comprised of many parts that work together.
- Systems are interrelated.
- Systems exist everywhere.
- Systems are made up of many systems.
- Systems have many parts, objects, or components that are organized to form a whole.
- Systems are dependent upon other systems.
- Some systems are closed and some are open.

FIGURE 4–2. Statement Listing Attributes Identified from Standards Bundled Under Systems

Students will

- Describe the structure of the parts and how they relate to the system.
- Describe the function of the parts and how they relate to the system.
- Justify the importance of various parts of a system.
- Provide evidence that parts and subsystems work together to create a system.
- Provide evidence and demonstrate how systems have been enhanced or improved through researching and studying their parts.

These mutual umbrella expectations are important because they will become the cornerstone for assessment in and across all content areas. Moreover, to avoid drifting from the conceptual view of the standards and creating a disjointed unit, they should connect to all content area expectations.

Additional assistance in developing student expectations is often available from state departments of education. Several states such as Ohio and New Mexico have developed benchmarks, which are published on their websites. Indicators and content performance standards are often available, also. Read the fine print carefully, because some of these descriptors are written as the minimum expectation levels. In most cases, it is our responsibility to enrich our expectations to reflect a higher level of learning for students.

Once the umbrella statement and mutual umbrella expectations are developed, they must evolve into interesting and relevant questions. Let's examine Figure 4–2 again to see how the middle-school teachers crafted their questions to align with the mutual umbrella expectations. The teachers were able to discern the essence of the standards by finding the most common attributes in the bundled standards. The following example illustrates that the teachers found that *the parts of a system* was a more common conceptual theme than *how systems interrelate* or than that *some systems are closed and some are open*. They turned the student expectations into the following list of possible umbrella questions:

- How do I perform as a part of the different systems within my life?
- How am I a part of different systems?
- How do the parts of a system affect me?
- How do I play a role in the systems in which I am affected?
- Which systems am I a part of?
- What part do I play in different systems?
- Which systems have parts that don't affect me?
- How do the different parts of a system work together to benefit me?
- How do the different parts that work together within a system perform a function that affects me?

Although the teachers were new to this process, it didn't take them long to develop this list and to craft their possible umbrella questions into a few that will frame their unit of study. They will continue to refine their questions, but they believe that the following umbrella questions accurately reflect what is important about their standards:

- How do the parts of a system work together to perform a function?
- What can I predict about different systems based on investigations of their parts?

These questions will now umbrella over their unit of study on *systems*. It is important to note that no content-specific concept or topic is mentioned in the umbrella questions; therefore, the questions are not specific to any one subject area. Additionally, nouns and concrete or tangible words are avoided since they limit the umbrella effect.

Think about the high school and the middle school umbrella questions. Both included some questions that connected to students in a personal way by using pronouns. To connect the questions to the student, include the pronouns *I*, *me*, or *my*, when it is reasonable to do so and when it doesn't deflect from the expectations for students.

Even though we have no memory of what the first year of our life was like, most of us know things about that time period. For example, people born in 1957 probably know that was the year the Soviet Union launched the satellite Sputnik. Most people can identify a picture of a vehicle manufactured in or near their birth year. The reason we can do this is because we have found a personal connection. We can assist students in finding some connections through personalizing questions when appropriate.

How Long Does an Umbrella Question Last?

Umbrella questions should be designed to umbrella an entire unit of study. They are not designed to frame a miniunit—which is simply a part of a larger unit. They are the broadest and most abstract type of questions that we will develop; yet they need to be extremely simple. Although there is no rule that specifies a length of time to use the same questions, four to twelve weeks is an average time frame.

Now What?

After the umbrella questions are developed, display them on the walls of your classroom along with the umbrella concept. Guide students to honor the focus of the question by referencing them to navigate student learning. When students are asked what they are learning they usually say things like fractions, the U.S. Constitution, or condensation. But, in classrooms across the country, I have seen different learning experiences for students. In a middle school in California, a tall, narrow pole stands in the corner of a classroom with the umbrella question crowning the top, and pictures, which students felt depicted the question, are hanging in a crowded column down the pole. In an elementary classroom on the other side of the country, an extra large, bright yellow umbrella hangs from the ceiling of the room. Dangling from the umbrella is the umbrella concept, the umbrella questions, and students' work that illustrates connections between content areas such as patterns in nature, patterns in design, patterns in population, and patterns in math. It is obvious that students are discovering the importance of the umbrella concepts and the umbrella questions. Additionally, when students are privately asked what they are learning, most reply by explaining the umbrella concept and how it fits into their learning such as "We are studying immigration and how it has changed the immigrants and our country" or "We are using patterns to solve problems and to identify the change of seasons." These teachers have succeeded in meshing the umbrella questions, the umbrella concepts, and the topics into a seamless framework allowing students to see a bigger picture. It is taking students to a deeper level of understanding.

Essential Questions Focus Topics and Content-Specific Concepts

The second type of question we will design is the *essential question*. Many experts have tried to define this type of question. In fact, there are so many different experts putting their spin on the definition that I find it confusing. A common vocabulary is essential to our work as educators, and the lack of one looms as a barrier to our learning. I have included a list of characteristics of essential questions. Of course, this is my spin, but it provides a common vocabulary to facilitate this process.

Essential Questions

- Are developed from the content-specific concepts, the topics, or both.
- Can provide a link between some content areas, but are not usually broad enough to umbrella all subjects.
- Scaffold down from the umbrella question becoming more content and topically specific.
- Provide a clear direction and focus.
- Cannot be answered with yes or no.
- Are challenging.
- Link the umbrella concept to the content-specific concepts and topics as appropriate.

Essential questions are devised through the same process used to develop the umbrella questions; however, now we include the content-specific concepts, topics, and essential content area student expectations. Begin by brainstorming statements derived from standards, mutual umbrella expectations, content-specific concepts, and topics to identify what is important about the content-specific concepts and the topics.

After the statement or statements are developed, each content area develops student expectations specific to its domain. This process continues until all subjects that are to be integrated have expectations. The essential expectations can cross content lines when a secure and natural fit is discovered. For example, a student expectation for the content areas of science and dance might be to use the elements of dance to illustrate cell movement. Finally, the essential expectations should interface with the umbrella concept of *systems*. The following expectations have been developed for the science thread of our middle school unit.

Final Science Expectation for cells, tissue, organs, organ systems, and living systems: Students will be able to make predictions about their future based on their own investigations of factors that can affect cell systems.

Essential Science Expectations

- Articulate what you already know about systems.
- Respond to umbrella questions.
- Articulate what you know about the system of the human body.
- Explain with a thorough description the definition of a cell.
- Identify animal cell parts.
- Describe the structure and function of animal cell parts.
- Compare and contrast animal and plant cell structures.
- Describe observations of an animal cell and plant cell using a microscope.
- Provide evidence of the essential elements of cell theory.
- Understand the structures and functions in an animal cell.
- Compare and contrast single-celled and multicelluar organisms.
- Identify differences among specialized cells (nerve, muscle, blood, skin, bone).
- Explain how cells have specialized functions and work together to form the levels of organization (cells, tissues, organs, organ system, organism).
- Explain how different cell processes function in order to sustain life (diffusion, osmosis, respiration, photosynthesis, reproduction, mitosis).
- Evaluate the importance of how different systems in a cell work together to perform cell process.
- Evaluate the importance of a body system in relation to the organism.
- Explain the effects of current cell research on diseases and treatment options.
- Predict what your future life will be like if cell research continues to improve treatment options.

Did you notice that content-specific concepts and topics were introduced in these essential expectations? In addition, topics and concepts were narrowed and focused. Even though topics are inherently narrower than concepts, it is still imperative to provide a focus for them.

Let's imagine for a moment that my social studies class is about to study the topic of Ancient Rome. Since I know we would not do without a conceptual focus, how will I focus their learning when there are so many directions that I can take?

- pagans, Christians, Jews (Roman gods and Christianity)
- roads, bridges, aqueducts, architecture, technology
- Mark Anthony, Julius Caesar
- geographical location and attributes (rivers, valleys)
- invasions, battles, wars
- the rise and fall of the Roman Empire

My responsibility as a teacher is to focus my class on what the standards say is important about Ancient Rome. I would need to seek answers for my focus by returning to my standards and the umbrella concept.

Imagine a topic such as World War I. How would you decide what the focus is for this topic? Why are we studying World War I? Is that topic mandated in the state standards through a stated topic? Do the standards take students beyond the topic? If standards tell us that World War I is essential for students to study, then we must uncover why it is important. Our responsibility is to teach what is stated in the standards and to take students beyond that mandate to a higher level of learning. Uncovering the importance of topics by looking beyond the standards is often the only way to ascertain what is so important about this war that we must guide students to discover it.

It is time to turn our attention back to our middle school example. Let's continue to build the foundation by developing essential questions in each content area for our unit of study on *systems*. Remember, essential questions are designed to frame the content-specific concepts, topics, and essential content area student expectations. See Figure 4–3 for some essential content areas questions for this middle school unit. The essential content area expectations and essential questions, all of which are standards-based, connect to the umbrella and thread through all content areas, thereby creating a focus for both the teachers and the students.

Designing essential questions is just the beginning. Once you have gained confidence in developing questions, it is the students' turn. Students may need some guidance initially, but give them the floor, and they will eventually dance.

Social Studies

- What systems can I identify in Ancient Rome, Greece, China, Africa, and India?
- What can I learn about each country by studying its systems?
- How do the political, economic, and social systems work together?
- How do discoveries from ancient cultures shape my beliefs about these civilizations?

Science

- What can I learn about my body by studying my parts?
- How will I know a cell if I meet one?
- How do systems in my body work together most efficiently in order to sustain life?
- How have discoveries about cells affected me?

Dance

- How was dance used by ancient cultures?
- How can I communicate using the elements of dance?
- How was space and energy used in different cultures?
- How can I change the movements and the time within a dance to reflect a different culture?

FIGURE 4–3. Essential Questions

How Long Do Essential Questions Last?

As a general rule, essential questions frame instruction anywhere between a few days and two to three weeks. However, exceptions to this rule certainly exist. Teachers decide how long a question retains its value in the context of their students' needs. These questions are designed to frame one or more strategies. They do not focus instruction for a short discussion or an activity, which only lasts one or two class periods. Ultimately, the teachers are the only ones who can decide when a question ceases to be beneficial to their students.

Guiding Questions: Questions That Guide
Short Instructional Periods

Although guiding questions are discussed in this chapter, they are not fully developed until the strategies and activities are identified. Guiding questions focus instruction for a short duration of time. In addition, they create a specific and immediate focus and purpose to a lesson. Guiding questions are named appropriately, because they guide small pieces of instruction. Guiding questions usually provide direction for a lesson. Examine the following guiding questions:

- What happens if I change a variable in this pattern?
- How are the patterns in this poem similar to the patterns in that poem?
- Which pattern best describes . . . ?
- How does the heat from this . . . compare to the heat from . . . ?
- What evidence supports this?
- How can I solve this problem?

Guiding questions not only guide instruction, but also give students a purpose. For example, before students read a story or passage, articulate a purpose for reading by posing questions to ponder and answer during the reading. Craft questions that nudge students to think at high levels, and that make them want to know the answer.

Pitfalls to Avoid

One school district conducts a Professional Growth Academy for new teachers. Four district administrators lead monthly workshops that are grounded in the research-based practices of curriculum, instruction, and assessment. Several sessions are focused specifically on questioning strategies. Teachers are taught to pause for a few seconds after asking a question and before calling on a student. Probing and follow-up questions are discussed. In addition, allowing equal access for all students is an important strategy that is explored during these sessions. Since they work so hard to model their strategies as they guide new teachers, you can imagine the surprise one administrator felt when she was found ignoring her own advice a few weeks later while demonstrating a lesson for teachers in their classrooms. She knew better, but she just wasn't paying enough attention to her questioning strategies. When she

Social Studies

- What systems can I identify in Ancient Rome, Greece, China, Africa, and India?
- What can I learn about each country by studying its systems?
- How do the political, economic, and social systems work together?
- How do discoveries from ancient cultures shape my beliefs about these civilizations?

Guiding Questions

- What questions would I ask about the customs of Africa if I could travel back in time?
- How can I answer the questions that I have drafted?
- What would my future look like if I were a Roman child?

Science

- What can I learn about my body by studying my parts?
- How will I know a cell if I meet one?
- How do systems in my body work together most efficiently in order to sustain life?
- How have discoveries about cells affected me?

Guiding Questions

- How do the cell structures function as a system?
- How can I tell if it is a plant cell or an animal cell?
- Can I sort cells?
- What systems are inside of a cell?
- How do systems interact to perform necessary life functions?

Dance

- How was dance used by ancient cultures?
- How can I communicate using the elements of dance?
- How was space and energy used in ancient cultures?
- How can I change the movements and the time within a dance to reflect a different culture?

Guiding Questions

- How can I choreograph a dance that depicts a story?
- What might the energy in a dance tell me about the purpose of a dance?
- If I were to dance in Africa, on what occasions might I perform?

FIGURE 4–4. Guiding Questions Added to Unit

realized what she was doing, she was embarrassed. After the lesson, she turned this mistake into a lesson for the teachers for whom she was modeling. She pointed out what her mistake was and explained that she was not practicing the expectations of her district. How often do we find ourselves talking the talk, but not walking the walk? Become familiar with appropriate types of questions and good questioning strategies.

Summing Up

Before moving to the next chapter, let's take a holistic peek at the *Essential Questions* in Figure 4–4 to see the progress made to the foundation of the middle school example. Some guiding questions have been included to illustrate what they might eventually look like.

We have learned that questions are a key ingredient to building a foundation worthy of our students. Although we tell our students that there are no dumb questions, we have learned that even a *smart* question will miss the target if it is not focused on the final expectations for students.

Terms to Remember

Essential Content Expectations: Student expectations developed in each content area from the standards, content-specific concepts, topics, and umbrella expectations. These expectations are the springboard for strategy development.

Essential Questions: Questions designed from topics and content-specific concepts embedded within the standards. They usually last from a few days to two or three weeks. These questions focus a miniunit.

Guiding Questions: Questions that guide instruction for a discussion, a lecture, a skill, or a minilesson. They focus small pieces of instruction and usually last for one or two class periods. These questions are standards-based.

Mutual Umbrella Expectations: Student expectations developed collaboratively to provide the connecting thread between content areas and assessments.

Umbrella Statements: Statements that capture the essence of the standards and clearly articulate a focus for teachers.

Umbrella Questions: Questions developed from the umbrella statements. They focus instruction and cover an entire unit of study, which can last from four to twelve weeks.

Further Reading

Hannel, G. I. 2001. *Highly Effective Questioning: Developing the Seven Steps to Critical Thinking.* 2d ed. Phoenix, AZ: Hannel Educational Consulting.

Simon, K. G. 2002. "The Blue Blood Is Bad, Right?" *Educational Leadership* 60 (6): 24–29.

5
Developing a Unit Framework

Classroom teachers examining standards and designing units side by side experience the same higher level thinking processes that they facilitate for their students such as accessing prior knowledge of content, of processes and of strategies, as well as making connections between standards which saves precious instructional time.

—Jamie Spugnardi, Regional Service Center director,
Kentucky Department of Education

Years ago, it was common for horse trainers to tame their horses with heavy hands on their whips. Today, trainers want their horses to work with them. Kentucky horseman Philip Whitney says, "Our goal is not to break the spirit, but to tame it. A horse with a broken spirit is dull and frightened, but a horse with a tame spirit is energetic, interested, and cooperative. Most of all, a tame, spirited horse is a joy to ride and work with."

Standards, like spiritless horses, are often somber and uninteresting. In the previous chapters, we captured the spirit of standards and tamed them. Questions were composed to ignite the innate wonder of our students, but now it is time to release that spirit onto a coherent pathway.

Planning Is Essential to Teaching at High Levels

Contrary to popular belief, teachers are human. As humans, they can easily become distracted, off task, or ineffective unless they have a definite plan to follow. This is especially true in the classroom. Planning for instruction is not usually a coveted task, but it is necessary. In fact, poor or inadequate planning usually translates into the same caliber instruction. Proper planning, however, easily converts into a footpath free of debris and obstacles. Since our students' success is dependent on what we value, we must value high-quality teaching.

Several years ago, a principal shared with me the story of one teacher who had used the same lesson plans for years. He said that every fall she erased the dates from the previous year and entered the current ones. Sadly,

I have observed teachers who were not designing lesson plans, who were designing inadequate ones, or who were using last year's plans without refinement or reflection—and I have observed the results of those teachers' lessons in the work of the students in those classrooms. It is important to understand how valuable planning is to student achievement.

Everyone Is Doing It: Standards-Based Units

Just as there are many ways to examine and bundle standards, there are multiple formats available for building a standards-based unit. Enter the keywords *standards-based units* on the Internet, and over 120,000 entries appear. It seems as if everyone is doing it.

Books, articles, and websites that outline methods and provide templates are in abundance. There are unit design formats based on thinking taxonomies, reform models, verbs, topics, issues, and questions—just to name a few. A few state departments of education like Vermont and Kentucky publish on their websites some suggestions and guidelines for developing a standards-based unit. Many of these templates and suggestions are excellent, but some are simply a traditional unit structure with a few additional spaces added for the standards. Many schools and districts have designed their own formats. The point is that no one has the one right format, but there are essential ingredients that make some better than others.

After years of assisting teachers develop units and lesson plans, I have come to realize that to ask teachers to create both a unit and lesson plans is asking too much, especially when we ask them to repeat that process every year. But, we can ask teachers to design a skeleton unit and to tweak their lesson plans each year. A skeleton unit allows teachers to develop lesson plans following an established pathway and based on the needs of their students. The first year, teachers design lesson plans; and each year thereafter, they will refine, adjust, and improve their plans and design additional activities to meet the different needs of their students. A skeleton unit is the pathway, which stays relatively constant, and the lesson plans are the footprints that will vary with students' needs.

The Structure of a Skeleton Unit: Exploring a Chain of Learning Links

A *skeleton unit* is a unit framework organized in a specific format. The organization or format of the unit is designed around what we know about how students learn. The following concepts or principles suggest how the skeleton unit is planned to complement how students learn.

- Activating prior knowledge
- Eliminating misconceptions
- Connecting new learning to prior knowledge
- Creating interest and motivating students
- Delving into research, inquiry, and investigation, which assists students to discover and uncover learning
- Connecting learning in relevant ways—across content lines and into the lives of students
- Extending learning to new situations
- Reflecting on learning

Skeleton units are organized around these principles, as well as other brain-based theories that are considered during the design of the unit.

A skeleton unit is not one long unit; rather, it is a group of miniunits placed strategically so that one miniunit scaffolds to the next. One miniunit might eventually connect to one or two additional miniunits to form the chain, or it could stand alone as the only miniunit within a skeleton unit.

Imagine a chain with multiple links. The entire chain represents a skeleton unit, and each link represents one miniunit or chunk of learning attaching to the link before it to scaffold learning. The umbrella concept, which is the chain, threads through each link. By following the learning links, we are less likely to deviate from what we know about student learning.

Learning Link: Activating, Assessing, Eliminating, Engaging
The chain represents the umbrella concept, the mutual umbrella expectations, the umbrella questions, and this chain threads through all of the links. When introducing the first sequence in a link, the umbrella concept, questions, and mutual umbrella expectations must be introduced and integrated into the essential content areas. In this way, we are showing students the big picture first.

There is a three-part sequence that we follow to open the initial link (or miniunit): Begin by

1. Activating and accessing prior knowledge.
2. Eliminating misconceptions.
3. Creating an interesting and engaging hook.

Although most teachers recognize that it is important to use these three elements in their lesson and unit designs, frequently and inadvertently, one or more is omitted such as accessing prior knowledge. Zemelman, Daniels, and Hyde noted in their book *Best Practice: New Standards for Teaching and Learning in America's Schools*, "By drawing out and then building on this prior knowledge that children bring to school, we can help them discover . . ." (1998, 143). They also suggest that we introduce the whole, which is our umbrella, rather than introduce and teach our content in isolated parts, "When the 'big picture' is put off until later, later often never comes" (1998, 10).

The first sequence in a skeleton unit is *Learning Link: Activating, Assessing, Eliminating, Engaging*. To begin this learning link, teachers design strategies to introduce the miniunit, activate and assess prior knowledge about the umbrella concept and the umbrella questions as well as the essential questions, eliminate misconceptions, and create an interesting and engaging hook. For example, a strategy to activate and assess prior knowledge around the umbrella concept of *discoveries* might be for the teacher to provide an example of a discovery and have the students brainstorm several discoveries. Then, to eliminate misconceptions, the teacher would guide students to uncover if their discoveries were correct. To hook students, teachers would pose a question to pique their interest.

In addition to the principles of accessing, eliminating, and creating a hook, the process of exploration, investigation, and discovery of the content-specific concepts, topics, and skills will begin in this sequence. For example, under the umbrella concept of *discoveries*, the teacher would activate and assess their students' prior knowledge, eliminate misconceptions that students have, and create an engaging hook for the content-specific concepts that are being introduced such as *natural resources*. Then we would begin a voyage of uncovering a deeper level of learning by getting started in the next phase of the link by exploring the *discoveries* of *natural resources*. Let's examine the opening sequence of the link.

Learning Link: Activating, Accessing, Eliminating, Engaging

1. Introduce the umbrella concept, umbrella and essential questions, content-specific concepts, topics, mutual umbrella expectations, and essential content expectations.
2. Activate and assess prior knowledge.
3. Eliminate misconceptions.
4. Create an interesting and engaging hook to capture and motivate students.
5. Begin the exploration of concepts, topics, and skills.

Persistent Exploration

The next sequence within this same link will guide students to continue exploring and discovering. This learning link is called *Persistent Exploration*, and it can be repeated indefinitely as we guide students through the pathway into a deeper level of learning. Imagine that through the umbrella concept of *discoveries* students were exploring natural resources in their world. In Persistent Exploration, we might design strategies for students to investigate how natural resources were discovered, what they are used for, and to justify their importance with evidence. Every strategy would be designed to take students a little deeper into this exploration. Examine the second sequence of this learning link.

Persistent Explorations

- Persistent Exploration 1.1
- Persistent Exploration 1.2
- Persistent Exploration 1.3

Notice that there is a number after each bulleted Persistent Exploration. The first number tells that it belongs to the first learning link, Learning Link One, and the second number indicates the order of the scaffolding through the Persistent Explorations. There can be several sequential layers of learning—each building on and deepening student learning. For example, the content of this book might be broken down into scaffolding through Persistent Explorations.

- *Persistent Exploration 1.1*
  Umbrella Concepts, Content-Specific Concepts, Topics
- *Persistent Exploration 1.2*
  Study of Bundling and Cross-Bundling
- *Persistent Exploration 1.3*
  Umbrella, Essential, and Guiding Questions and Student
  Expectations

Each Persistent Exploration contains a chunk of learning connected to and scaffolded from the previous chunk.

Learning Link: Internalizing, Reflecting, Connecting, Extending
This is the closing sequence of the same link. See how it unfolds:

1. Reflect on new learning.
2. Apply new learning by connecting it to something relevant.
3. Use new learning to solve problems, create, design, and justify.

We close each link by allowing students to articulate the connections they made during their voyage and by nudging students to make new connections such as how *discoveries* of *natural resources* are still being made today. This link also provides a springboard for students' reflections and extensions. How can students extend their learning? What did students learn? Can students justify the relevancy of this learning? Within this learning link, it is important for students to make lasting connections, reflect on their learning, extend their learning, and to see how their learning will be beneficial. This link is designed to assist students in internalizing their own learning and understanding how it transcends subject lines and real-world boundaries to become applicable to their lives.

Repeating the Links

All of these components create one learning link or one miniunit. These links or miniunits are strategically threaded into our umbrella chain to form a skeleton unit. The umbrella is continually addressed in every link. Each link added to the chain is designed using the learning links model:

1. Learning Link: Activating, Accessing, Eliminating, Engaging
2. Learning Link: Persistent Exploration (can have multiple layers)
3. Learning Link: Internalizing, Reflecting, Connecting, Extending

There may be one link (miniunit), or there may be many links (miniunits) within one skeleton unit. Regardless of the number of links, the sequence is repeated with each new link.

The Repeating Sequence: The Learning Chain and Its Links

To understand the concept of repeating links on the chain of learning, inspect the following outline. It illustrates how the learning links are repeated until students reach the final essential content expectations and the final mutual umbrella expectations.

Learning Link One

Learning Link One: Activating, Accessing, Eliminating, Engaging
Learning Link One: Persistent Exploration (can have multiple layers)

Persistent Exploration 1.1
Persistent Exploration 1.2
Persistent Exploration 1.3

Learning Link One: Internalizing, Reflecting, Connecting, Extending

Learning Link Two

>   Learning Link Two: Activating, Accessing, Eliminating, Engaging
>   Learning Link Two: Persistent Exploration (can have multiple layers)
>>   Persistent Exploration 2.1
>>   Persistent Exploration 2.2
>   Learning Link Two: Internalizing, Reflecting, Connecting, Extending

Links continue to be added to the chain as new miniunits are scaffolded from the previous one. There may be a few large links, several small links, or a combination of both within every umbrella chain since skeleton units are constructed from multiple miniunits that become the strategically designed pathway. Each link or miniunit will be part of the pathway for instruction, and each may take from several days to several weeks to complete.

The Strategic Use of Strategies

Strategies that reflect the common expectations are the final component in our skeleton unit infrastructure. Designed and strategically placed into a logical, sequential, and scaffolding pathway, strategies patiently wait to explode into multifaceted activities in future lesson plans.

Common Vocabulary

Before we examine a skeleton unit and its structure, it is important to differentiate between a strategy and an activity. A mutual understanding and a common vocabulary are vital. The terms *strategy* and *activity* have been used interchangeably for many years. Sometimes, educators confuse the idea of strategies with activities. There is, however, a difference.

An activity is incorporated within a unit to keep students active and engaged, but a strategy is designed to assist students in reaching their learning goals. *The American Heritage College Dictionary*, third edition (1997) defines an activity as, "an educational procedure intended to stimulate learning through experience" (14). Because activities are components of a larger strategy, there may be one or many activities with a strategy.

A strategy is defined as, "intended to accomplish a specific goal" (*The American Heritage Dictionary* 1997, 1342). With a strategy, we have intentionally calculated the outcomes. The synonyms for a strategy—*design, scheme, craft, calculate,* and *plan*— underscore the meaning of planning a pathway.

In a skeleton unit, we will design strategies. The activities will be planned later within the lesson plans. Strategies are the plan; activities are steps in the plan. Strategies frame the pathway for learning; activities are the experiences along the path. An example of an isolated activity might be a reading assignment of pages 1 through 3 of a story. The strategy would include the activity, but also additional activities, too. Examine the following strategy. How many embedded activities can you identify within this brief strategy?

> *Design a model of a system and articulate the function of the parts of the system.*

> Using this strategy, an activity might be developed for students to
> 1. Select a system to use in this design. Possible activities: Cooperatively group students (three to a group), and have them use magazines or other resources to select a system.
> 2. Construct the identified system using clay, poster board, or other materials.
> 3. Research the parts of the system.
> 4. Compare and contrast the function of the parts of a system by responding to an open response question.
> 5. Use a rubric to peer assess the models through jigsaw groups.

Understanding the difference between a strategy and an activity is important because in a skeleton unit, we are looking holistically at a pathway built from strategies, not necessarily at the individual activities that reside within these strategies. This is sometimes a frustrating task because many teachers have only dealt with activities isolated from the strategies.

Often it is difficult for teachers to describe strategies because they are accustomed to dealing with only the activities. They have been inundated with new activities, but few teachers have learned to place these tools within strategies—in other words, within a strategic plan.

A Science Skeleton Unit

Since teachers also use prior knowledge to connect with new learning, ideas for activities and guiding questions will naturally emerge while strategies are being designed. It is impossible for an experienced teacher to design strategies without thinking of activities and guiding questions drawn from past professional experiences or imagining new ones that might guide students to a deeper understanding. These ideas are essential ingredients for expanding skeleton units into lesson plans. When they emerge, and they will, it is okay to include them as possible activities and guiding questions within the design. Although all activities are expanded and refined during the design of the lesson plan, it is important to include professional experience in the process by making note of emerging ideas; after all, the final design hinges upon teachers integrating their current knowledge with their new learning.

With that in mind, let's examine the science skeleton unit in Figures 5–1 through 5–4. Carefully study how the questions guide the strategies and how the pathway is sequenced from the strategies. Additionally, notice the addition of possible activities and potential guiding questions.

Strategies guide the next sequential step and provide a framework for designing lesson plans while providing a clear view to the next and then final step. When I was in college, I was taught to write lesson plans by listing the objectives for the lesson and by designing activities for those objectives. This design perpetuated my dealing in isolation with activities and individual lessons. There was little consideration given to next week or the end of the unit since it usually coincided with the end of the textbook chapter. By using strategies that are purposefully scaffolded, we build a skeleton plan that will be developed more fully as we gain insight into the needs of our students, but it is based on our standards and what was embedded within or beyond them.

We analyzed the frame of the skeleton unit in the content area of science because it is an exemplar of how a skeleton unit can embody broad strategies in a logical pathway for student learning. These strategies are the springboard for future lesson plans. While continuing this process for other content areas, teachers who are not working collaboratively should proceed alone. The process is important for all teachers regardless of whether they teach only one or two content areas, are self-contained, or are departmentalized.

Why Skeleton Units?

While we have discussed several reasons to work through this process, it is important to explore a few more. Teachers have trouble finding the time to plan one week in advance, much less develop full-blown units. By devoting time up front to developing a pathway, teachers can unfold the unit through lesson plan development and spread their work time over many months. Why, you might ask, can the whole unit not be developed through lesson plans? Without a clearly visible pathway, there is a tendency to design lessons in isolation, to use a textbook or other resources as the pathway rather than the standards, to design the lessons and then search for standards that match, and finally, because it is easy, to design a wooden, inflexible unit with little to no consideration given to individual student needs.

Learning Link One: Activating, Assessing, Eliminating, Engaging

Umbrella Concept: Systems
Umbrella Questions (Hook)
- How do the parts of a system work together to perform a function?
- What can I predict about different systems based on investigations of their parts?

Mutual Umbrella Expectations
- Identify a variety of systems and their parts.
- Describe the structure of the parts and how they relate to the system.
- Describe the function of the parts and how they relate to the system.
- Justify the importance of various parts of a system.
- Provide evidence that parts and subsystems work together to create a system.
- Provide evidence and demonstrate how systems have been enhanced or improved through researching their parts.

Final Science Expectations
- Students will be able to make predictions about their future based on their own investigations of factors that can affect cell systems.

Essential Science Expectations
- Articulate what you already know about systems.
- Respond to umbrella questions (assessing prior knowledge).
- Articulate what you know and what you want to know about the system of the human body.

Concepts: systems, living systems
Topics: (shared by all content areas: various systems, that is, factories, schools, bicycles)

Essential Science Question (Hook)
- What can I learn about my body by studying my parts?

Student Strategies
1. Articulate a system through various modes. (Can you describe what a system is?)
   Possible Activities: Group discussion of what a system is and examples of systems.
2. Identify the parts and understand their importance to the whole system. (Can you articulate the different parts and their function in a system?)
   Possible Activities: Group students (three to a group) and give each group pictures of different systems. Students will identify parts and describe their importance (student choice).
3. Articulate what you know about the human body system.
   Possible Activities: In groups, create a graphic organizer of information about human body systems (examples, functions, parts, etc.). Then, generate a list of questions you want answered during this unit.

Approximate Timeline: 1 to 2 days

FIGURE 5–1. Middle School Science Skeleton Unit

Learning Link One: Persistent Exploration 1.1

Essential Question (Hook)
- How will I know a cell if I meet one?

Possible Guiding Questions
- What will my cells contain?
- How do the cell structures function as a system?
- How can I tell if it is a plant cell or an animal cell?

Essential Learning: The cell is the basic unit of most living things. Differentiate between plant and animal cells.

Essential Science Expectations
1. Articulate what you know about the system of the human body.
2. Explain with a thorough description the definition of a cell.
3. Identify animal cell parts.
4. Describe the structure and function of animal cell parts.
5. Compare/contrast animal and plant cell structures.
6. Describe observations of an animal cell and plant cell using a microscope.
7. Provide evidence of the essential elements of cell theory.
8. Understand the structures and functions in an animal cell (product or performance).

Concepts: organism, organelles, cell, systems
Topics: cell membrane, cytoplasm, nucleus, nuclear membrane, nucleolus, vacuole, Golgi body, mitochondria, endoplasmic reticulum, ribosomes, plant cells, cell wall, chloroplast, human body system, lysosome

---

Student Strategies: Explain prior knowledge of the human body system.
Assessment: What do you know about the body system?
Possible Activities: Label as many parts of the body system as possible and describe function of each.

Possible Activities
1. Explain what cells are. (Can you accurately name the parts?)
2. Pre-test (What is a cell? What parts make up a cell?), determine examples of things that are and are not made up of cells, video about cells with quiz afterward, and articulate in science log the definition of a cell.
3. Design a model of a cell and describe its structure and function. (Did you realistically depict a cell in your model?)
   Possible Activities: Create a model of a cell using paper, clay, or other materials, or draw, label, or design a cell and label its parts.
4. Organize information about structures and their functions. (Can you tell why these structures are important to the cell?)

FIGURE 5–2. Middle School Science Skeleton Unit

continued

Possible Activities: Design a book with diagrams and information in a story form about cell parts and functions. (Follow scoring guide to meet requirements.)

5. Observe types of cells and identify cell structures. (What makes plant and animal cells different?)

   Possible Activities: Draw models of cells and label their structures. Compare and contrast three similarities and three differences. Take an imaginary trip through cells using candy to represent structures of the cell. Write a travel log in a science journal about trip.

6. Research the parts of the cell theory. (Why is each statement included in the cell theory?)

   Possible Activities: In groups, analyze importance of one assigned part of cell theory and explain to class.

7. Compare parts of a cell to parts of another system in the world. (What similarities do the parts of a cell have with a factory, city, or school?)

   Possible Activities: Open response—choose three structures of a cell and explain their functions. Then, compare each structure to parts of a city, factory, or school. (Use rubric as a guide.)

8. Articulate what you have learned about structures and functions in the cell. (Can you explain how all structures in the system of a cell work together to perform necessary life functions?)

   Possible Activities: In groups, create a song to a familiar tune about the structures of a cell and its functions.

FIGURE 5–2. *continued*

Persistent Exploration 1.2

Essential Question (Hook)
- How do systems in my body work together most efficiently in order to sustain life?

Possible Guiding Questions
- Can I sort cells?
- What systems are inside of a cell?
- How do systems interact to perform necessary life processes?

Essential Learning: Differentiate between multicellular and single-celled organisms, and know that most organisms are single-celled, understand the processes of respiration, growth, reproduction, removal of wastes, and cellular transport.

Essential Science Expectations
- Compare/contrast single-celled and multicellular organisms.
- Identify differences among specialized cells (nerve, muscle, blood, skin, bone).
- Explain how cells have specialized functions and work together to form the levels of organization (cells, tissues, organs, organ system, organism).
- Explain how different cell processes function in order to sustain life (diffusion, osmosis, respiration, photosynthesis, reproduction, mitosis).
- Evaluate the importance of how different systems in a cell work together to perform cell processes.

Concepts: organism, multicellular organism, single-celled organism, bacteria, fungi, aerobic, anaerobic, respiration, asexual reproduction, sexual reproduction, osmosis, diffusion, mitosis, levels of organization, specialization, photosynthesis, processes
Topics: bacteria, fungi

Student Strategies
1. Observe examples of single-celled and multicellular organisms. (What are the differences and similarities?)
   Possible Activities: Discuss similarities and differences in groups, create a graphic organizer.
2. Organize information about different types of animal cells and their functions. (How are the types of cells specialized to perform different tasks in a system?)
   Possible Activities: Create a booklet of different types of animal cells with drawings and notes about their functions. Choose a type of cell, draw a model, and explain how it helps to carry out life functions.
3. Analyze different body systems and the levels of organization. (How are cells specialized?)
   Possible Activities: In groups, choose a body system and create a diagram of the levels of organization specific for that body system. Also, describe the specific functions of the system and write a brief explanation of how the parts of the system work together. Present to the class.

FIGURE 5–3. Middle School Science Skeleton Unit   *continued*

4. Demonstrate understanding of different cell processes. (How do the cell processes work? Why are they necessary for life?)
   Possible Activities: In groups, create a graphic organizer with information about each process. Create a demonstration of how an assigned process works using props, other students, signs, or other ideas. (Use scoring guide to meet requirements.) Perform a dance that models mitosis or create a model using pipe cleaners, sticks, or other materials.
5. Articulate what you have learned about how systems of a cell perform necessary life processes and why they are important. (How are processes performed within the system of a cell and what is the significance of these processes?)
   Possible Activities: Open response—choose a process and explain how a cell system performs the process and why it is important. (Follow rubric.)

Approximate Timeline: 3 weeks

FIGURE 5–3. *continued*

Learning Link One: Internalizing, Reflecting, Connecting, Extending

Essential Question (Hook)
- How have discoveries about cells affected me?

Guiding Questions
- Why is the interaction of my body system important?
- How have discoveries in cell research affected cell diseases and treatment options?
- What can I predict about my future based on further improvements in treatment of cell diseases?

Essential Learning: Body systems interact. Discoveries in cell research have affected the seriousness of cell diseases. The future can have positive and/or negative effects because of improvements in treatments for cell diseases.

Essential Science Expectations
- Evaluate importance of a body system in relation to the organism.
- Explain the effects of current cell research on diseases and treatment options.
- Predict what your future life will be like in the world if cell research continues to improve treatment options.

Concepts: organ systems, cells
Topics: cell diseases, treatments

Student Strategies
1. Articulate what you have learned about the importance of body systems to the organism. (Is one system more important than others?)
   Possible Activities: Choose a body system and evaluate the importance of that system to the organism as a whole.
2. Demonstrate understanding of effects of cell research on organisms. (How has cell research affected life?)
   Possible Activities: In groups, investigate how cell research has affected treatment options (cancer, organ transplants, gene therapy) for a cell disease and present information in some form (presentation, written, diagrams, display, or other).
3. Based on your investigations of cell research, predict what your future will be like if current research continues to show improvements in treatment options. (How do you view your future if treatment options continue to improve?)
   Possible Activities: Open response—predict what your future life and world may be like if research continues to improve treatment options for cell diseases. (Use rubric as a guide.)

Approximate Timeline: 1 week

Science Strand by Bethany Hill, middle school science teacher

FIGURE 5–4. Middle School Science Skeleton Unit

Flexibility, in and of itself, is an important reason to develop the lesson plans as we work through a unit of study. Since students arrive at our doorstep with different experiences, with unique learning styles, at different stages of cognitive development, and with special needs, we must design our lessons to address these differences. Additionally, new teachers have few experiences to draw from to design a unit. They need to acclimate themselves to what is *usually* developmentally appropriate for this age student.

A skeleton unit inherently is more flexible than a textbook and other resources because the lesson plans are based on the current needs of your students this year and the needs of future students. Most units and textbooks are somewhat concrete in their design, but since the teachers are the authors of the skeleton units and lesson plans, they are more comfortable acting as editors.

Exploring Lesson Planning

Lesson planning is an important process on the path to facilitating high levels of student learning. There is little continuity across the nation in expectations for lesson plans. I am sure that you have seen some lesson plans that look exactly the same each day except that the page numbers from the textbook have changed. On the other hand, you have probably seen high-quality plans that include many essential components.

We will not explore lesson plans in depth, but it would be negligent not to look at some essential elements of lesson planning since they are the footprints of our skeleton units. What do you know about developing a high-quality lesson plan? Do you believe that we should develop one lesson plan for each day of the week? Have you ever been told that one lesson plan can last more than one class period? What elements of instruction are so important that they cannot be omitted from a lesson plan?

Historically, lesson plan books were distributed to teachers in formats that were typically designed with a box per day per subject area. Anyone who has been in education for even a short period of time recognizes "the plan book." In reality, a good lesson may actually last one class period, but more often than not, it will last several class periods. If you use the box format, I bet you have written the word *continue* in some of those boxes. Lesson plans do not fit neatly into a small box each day. In other words, the best lesson plan format should allow for flexibility and should be designed in a format that allows you to enter the time frame rather than rewriting the plan each day or week.

What we have learned from brain research has given us great insight into how students learn. This too should be incorporated into our lesson planning process. Just as we accessed prior knowledge when we introduced the umbrella and the essential content knowledge, we embed the same principle into lesson plans each time we introduce new concepts, skills, or topics. Moreover, we need to include other, similar principles from our skeleton unit design into our lesson plans such as creating a hook, reflecting, connecting, allowing for inquiry and discovery, recognizing continuous assessment, developing lesson outcomes, and asking questions that guide instruction, which are the guiding questions. Maybe you have noticed by now that lesson plans are designed much like our chain of learning within our skeleton unit.

Students learn at high levels when teachers

- Assess prior knowledge linking to umbrella concept and questions and mutual umbrella expectations.
- Assess prior content knowledge.
- Create and capture students' attention such as an emotional or interest-driven hook.
- Link student expectations to standards and align with strategies, activities, skills, and assessments.
- Create assessments that are continuous, developmentally appropriate, and authentic and that are based on clearly defined criteria such as a scoring guide or rubric.
- Develop strategies, activities, expectations, and umbrella, essential, and guiding questions that promote higher order thinking.
- Connect learning to students' lives in a relevant and personal way.
- Provide opportunities within the activities and lessons for multiple modes of learning.
- Provide choices for students in learning and in demonstration of learning.
- Include process skills such as observing, communicating, and listening.
- Encourage discovery through research, inquiry, investigation, and testing hypothesis.
- Provide time for practice.
- Expand understanding and application by asking students to draw conclusions, design experiments, design projects, ask and answer questions, make connections, and assess self and peers.

- Embed reflection into learning for students and for teacher.

These are the tools that we must build into lesson plans. Now, can all of that fit in one of those boxes? No. Because it takes time to implement a quality lesson, the box method is antiquated. Today, we recognize that lesson plans are designed with the students as the focus and not the lesson plan book.

Clasping the Chain into a Circle

Did you notice that we never connected our learning chain into a complete circle? The final snap that secures the chain into a circle is examining student work. To guide instruction and close the last gap, we must include this clasp in the chain. In fact, it should occur frequently throughout the chain. Examining student work is imperative because it propels the next lesson. What we learn about our own work and the work of our students will guide our instruction in multiple ways. Looking at student work will allow teachers to develop next steps and to recognize when strategies and activities need to be refined, adjusted, added, or omitted for student success.

Assessing the Skeleton Unit

Now that the standards are tamed and the skeleton unit is complete, lesson plans will be designed. When developing lesson plans from each of the strategies, it is important to identify emerging trends in the activities being designed such as a lack of student groupings or the too frequent use of direct instruction. By monitoring and staying cognizant of including a variety of activities, we can modify any unwanted trend early in the process. Using the Unit Assessment Matrix in Figure 5–5, teachers can self-assess their own units as they unfold. This tool provides teachers a lens to critique their own work holistically. It is easy to complete the matrix as each lesson plan is developed from the skeleton unit.

To use this matrix, place a check mark in the box beside all instructional techniques that are included within a strategy. Work through the process as you look at the following example. In the column under Strategy 1, check all techniques that are found in the activities.

Strategy: Observe examples of single-celled and multicelluar organisms.

Activities

In cooperative groups of three:
  1. Examine a single-celled and a multicelluar organism.
  2. Discuss and make notes of the differences.

Strategy		1	2	3	4	5	6	7	8	9	10	11	12	13	14
Pairs	Student Groupings														
Cooperative groups															
Small sroups															
Peer tutors															
Individual															
Whole group															
Jigsaw															
Carousel															
Other (list)															
Howard Gardner's Multiple Intelligences	Verbal														
	Mathematical														
	Musical														
	Kinesthetic														
	Spatial														
	Intrapersonal														
	Interpersonal														
Compare/contrast	Research-Based Instruction														
Modeling writing															
Metaphors															
Predicting and hypothesizing															
Symbolic representations															
Mnemonic devices															
Questions															
Advanced or graphic organizers															
Manipulatives															
Classifying or sequencing															
Modeling															
Reading to students															
Conferencing															
Accessing prior knowledge															
Student reflection															
Research															
Problem solving															
Connecting to real life															
Connecting to other content															
Analogies															
Practice															

FIGURE 5–5. Unit Assessment Matrix

continued

Strategy		1	2	3	4	5	6	7	8	9	10	11	12	13	14
Student choice provided	Research-Based Instruction														
Technology embedded (list)															
Read-aloud															
Homework															
Journals															
Thinking about thinking															
Peer evaluations															
Rubrics/scoring guide															
Writing for real audiences															
Multiple resources															
Student experiments															
Assessment Strategies	Writing														
	Journals														
	Inquiry														
	Product														
	Performance														
	Portfolio														
	Investigation														
	Observation														
	Anecdotal records														
	Conferencing														
	Teacher-made test														
	Textbook test														
	Evidence gathering clearly defined														
Lecture	Diminishing Strategies														
Direct instruction															
Teacher's choice															
Writing without a purpose															
Sharing without a purpose															
No evidence gathering															

FIGURE 5–5. *continued*

3. Create a graphic organizer to compare and contrast the differences.

In pairs
    4. Partner with someone from another group and peer assess your organizer using a scoring guide.

Individually
    5. Respond to an open response question that asks for evidence of the differences.

You could have placed a check mark beside all of the following instructional techniques found in Strategy 1:

Pairs	Symbolic representations
Cooperative groups	Questions (guiding, essential, and umbrella)
Individual	Advanced or graphic organizers
Verbal	Manipulatives
Kinesthetic	Technology embedded (microscope)
Spatial	Rubrics/Scoring guide
Interpersonal	Writing
Intrapersonal	Product
Compare and contrast	Observation

Most teachers are surprised at how easy it is to see the big picture using this checklist. It requires very little time to complete—usually less than a minute per strategy and accompanying activities—and the benefits are mammoth.

Imagine that lesson plans are developed for the first three strategies. When you use a checklist, you might note that a pattern is emerging in the lack of writing planned for students. This early in the unit, it would not be a problem for you to begin to embed writing in future activities, but if the end of the unit is reached before this is noticed, valuable time is wasted. Recognizing these trends early allows plenty of time to include a larger variety of experiences or even to begin omitting some of the experiences that are not considered a best practice in instruction.

Assessing the Use of Standards

Ideally, a school will have a software program for lesson planning. However, the reality is that most schools do not value lesson planning to that extent. Some of these software programs are able to track the standards in each lesson plan and create reports that inform the teachers when standards have been addressed, how often, at what grade level, in what context, and at what depth standards were explored. Some of these software programs will not allow teachers to create a lesson without first identifying the standards the lesson will be based on.

There are also software programs that do everything for teachers such as create units and lessons. Knowing that the process is as important as the product if true systemic change is desired in a school, I find these types of programs are more of a bandage rather than a long-term shift in teachers' thinking about standards. These types of programs depend on the standards themselves. Without looking within and beyond the standards, we are using just a list of content, skills, or someone else's units to design our lessons and nothing has changed. In these cases, we might as well use textbooks.

The Standards Checklist in Figure 5–6 is used in lieu of a software program that teachers use to build their own lessons based on their own skeleton units. Because most schools have not invested in such software, this checklist assists teachers in accounting for all standards. Teachers know the needs of their students, but often they depend on the authors of textbooks, units, resource manuals, software, and other teachers to be the professional in their classroom by telling them that materials are already aligned with standards. If teachers had the time to dig deeply, they would find that that may not always be true. The checklist is used to check standards as they are addressed within each strategy along the pathway. For schools that have developed several small standards from larger standards, it is imperative to use some form of standards tracking system because of the sheer number of them. From the bundled and sorted standards, it is not difficult to design this type of checklist. Using this checklist helps avoid unintentionally omitting standards from the unit design. In addition, documentation of a direct link from each standard to a bundle, from bundle to unit design, and from unit design to lesson plan can be demonstrated.

This checklist can become an important document for tracking standards. Every time a standard is addressed, there is a record. Some state departments of educations are now performing audits on schools. In these audits, members of the audit team are specifically looking for the link between the standards and the lesson plans. With this method, audit team members can follow the thread from standards to students.

Standard		Strategy														
Umbrella concept: *Elements*		1	2	3	4	5	6	7	8	9	10	11	12	13	14	15
WR123	Use the elements of writing in all content areas		✓	✓	✓											
MA111	Create, recognize, extend, find, write, and apply rules for number patterns	✓								✓						✓
SC100	Identify the different layers of the Earth and explain their composition					✓	✓	✓	✓	✓						
SS188	Examine the basic components of the U.S. economic system						✓									

FIGURE 5–6. Standards Checklist

Pitfalls to Avoid

Reflecting is a natural part of life. Have you ever left a conversation saying to yourself, "I should have said this or not said that?" We inherently reflect when time allows. We learn from our reflections and are able to apply that learning in other situations. Teachers are becoming increasingly aware of the importance of student reflection, but they are forgetting their own need to reflect.

Put your skeleton unit in a three-ring binder divided into learning links. Include extra paper at the end of each lesson and label it Reflection as a reminder that reflection is necessary. Consider the following questions: How did the lesson go? How can I engage students more deeply? Did I omit essential learning? Was the strategy developmentally appropriate? What connections did students make? What improvements or refinements are needed? The point is to take the time to jot down some notes while they are fresh in your mind instead of waiting until next semester or next year when memories have faded. I know that I often have trouble remembering yesterday, much less last week and especially last year!

Summing Up

Skeleton units are different from the traditional design of a unit of study, a prefabricated unit, or a textbook. The major difference is that the actual lessons are designed gradually over time and as students' needs are identified instead of employing a prescribed set of activities. Each group of students who journey through the skeleton unit will help carve the refinements to lessons and strategies, and students who have a special need, from difficulty in mastering a skill to needing a more challenging discovery, will leave their prints in the skeleton unit. With each student or group of students, refinements and minilessons are added to meet individual and group needs, thus breathing life into the design. Skeleton units are a pathway linking standards, concepts, topics, skills, and student expectations to individual lesson plans while giving full consideration to the needs of our students. They do not supplant dynamic lesson plans and minilessons; rather, they dovetail to become a purposeful and articulated pathway for student learning that is based on your standards and directly on your students.

Terms to Remember

Activity: Engaging and interesting learning that allows students to experience the multiple parts of a strategy.

Chain of Learning: A thread that runs through all learning links and connects them to the umbrella concept, umbrella questions, and mutual umbrella expectations.

Essential Expectations: Student expectations aligned with content area standards and essential questions. Strategies are designed to assist students in meeting these expectations. Also referred to as *essential content expectations*.

Learning Links: A sequence in the chain of learning. Each link provides a structure for scaffolding learning while maintaining a focus on final expectations. They are designed based on available knowledge of how students learn. Learning Links are repeated over and over until closure is reached on a skeleton unit. A miniunit is usually one link. All links thread through the conceptual chain.

Mutual Umbrella Expectations: Student expectations designed from the umbrella concept and based on the standards within that bundle. Also referred to as *mutual expectations*.

Skeleton Unit: A unit framework aligned with standards that includes student expectations, questions that guide instruction, a conceptual umbrella, and broad strategies that create a clear pathway to develop lesson plans.

Strategy: A plan to take students to a deeper level of learning.

Further Reading

Allen, D. 1998. *Assessing Student Learning: From Grading to Understanding.* New York: Teachers College Press.

Blythe, T., D. Allen, and B. Schieffelin Powell. 1999. *Looking Together at Student Work: A Companion Guide to Assessing Student Learning.* New York: Teachers College Press.

Silver, H. F., R. Strong, and M. J. Perini. 2000. *So Each May Learn: Integrating Learning Styles and Multiple Intelligences.* Alexandria, VA: ASCD.

Zemelman, S., H. Daniels, and A. Hyde. 1998. *Best Practice: New Standards for Teaching and Learning in America's Schools.* 2d ed. Portsmouth, NH: Heinemann.

6

Developing a Curriculum Map

When I finished aligning my curriculum, I felt like I had accomplished a huge feat. I had unit frameworks and a direction for developing my lesson plans. Because I had already created the pathway for my students, I was able to organize my curriculum into a map in about half an hour. I discovered that a map was nothing more than a manifestation of my skeleton units. In the end, my units provided me with a blueprint of how to teach and assess my students while satisfying the state standards, and my map became a tool for communicating with parents, students, and other teachers.

—Jennifer Simonson, middle school teacher,
Vancouver, Washington

Curriculum mapping is all the rage. Many schools either have curriculum maps, or they have plans to develop them. On the other hand, there are schools that have developed curriculum maps, but they are not using them. Some state departments of education have endorsed mapping by including it as a component in their standards for school improvement, and some schools have mandated mapping as an ultimate goal. Schools are scrambling to get their maps in place for a variety of reasons. Regardless of the motivation, maps are in vogue, and it seems that is not going to change.

In this chapter, we

1. Explore a variety of organizational formats and several different interpretations of curriculum mapping.
2. Look at mapping in the context of taming the standards and learn how to preserve the alignment of the standards while developing a brief overview of what students will be studying.
3. Examine some curriculum maps that came out of our work.

Exploring Curriculum Maps

Heidi Hayes Jacobs explains in her book, *Mapping the Big Picture: Integrating Curriculum and Assessment K–12,* that curriculum mapping "is a procedure for collecting data about the actual curriculum in a school district using the school calendar as an organizer" (1997, 61). Jacobs outlines the two methods of collecting data to be included on a map. Teachers either use their state, district, or school standards to preplan their year, or they record the curriculum on the map as it is actually being taught. Jacobs believes that the most important function of a curriculum map is to promote conversations between teachers, students, and parents and to provide all teachers with a realistic view of what students are experiencing as they progress through school. She states, "The fundamental purpose of mapping is communication" (1997, 61).

Many schools began aligning their curriculum with the goal of neatly compartmentalizing their standards into a curriculum map. The process of designing a curriculum map was a major step for those schools. It was a first step in propelling a different type of thinking about how to organize mandated curriculum to increase student achievement.

Many teachers and administrators report that curriculum mapping prompted the first real conversations around alignment issues. In one middle school, all of the teachers attended a retreat for two days to map their curriculum. Prior to this, teachers usually went to their classrooms, closed their doors, and opened their textbooks. They mapped their instruction vertically over the three years that students attended their school, grades six, seven, and eight, and horizontally throughout each grade level. During this retreat, teachers gently nudged and challenged the placement of curriculum and its depth and breadth. The teachers reported that this one retreat changed their conversation forever. They also confessed that those maps were not as useful as their future alignment documents that resulted from their conversations. The process of mapping the curriculum can bring about real changes in the types of conversation teachers have. For this reason alone, curriculum mapping for some schools and teachers may be an excellent technique for improving the caliber of conversations.

Mapping can also ask teachers to look holistically at a school year. Curriculum mapping provides a new lens for teachers. As they map, they can view the sequence of the curriculum vertically and horizontally.

Indeed, curriculum maps serve a purpose—especially for those schools that have not developed standards-based units. Curriculum maps are wonderful tools for communicating with parents. Parents usually have no desire to read a complete unit of study, but they usually like an overview of what their child is learning, especially if it comes concise enough to fit on the front of their refrigerators.

Critical Components to Include in a Map

So what is this thing called a curriculum map? What are some elements that need to be included in order to accomplish this communication? Jacobs contends that the critical components for inclusion in a curriculum map are the

- processes and skills emphasized,
- content in terms of essential concepts and topics, or the content as examined in essential questions, and
- products and performances that are the assessments of learning. (1997, 8)

Have you visited many school or district websites lately? If so, you will find numerous examples of curriculum maps. Some maps have all the components and more advocated by the experts, and some are simply a list of topics to be taught each month. What you will not find are many examples of curriculum maps that cross subject lines to integrate the curriculum. And, if you do, it is unlikely that you will recognize many of them. Mapping is usually completed with little consideration of curriculum integration, and if the map is integrated, it is often invisible to all but the author.

Other observations that you might make while studying these curriculum maps are that standards are rarely linked to the map and that many maps are incomplete. Maybe standards are linked through another method, or perhaps there is no linkage at all. Additionally, many maps that are published appear to be incomplete. The section labeled *assessments* is often left totally or partially blank. Are these critical attributes in a map?

It is clear that Jacobs believes that assessments are a critical component of a curriculum map. Why then are so many maps published without the assessments developed? Teachers know the answer to this question. Assessments are extremely difficult to design without working through the standards and developing incremental student expectations. This may not be how the experts tell teachers to design assessments, but it is reality. During a recent work session, one teacher said, "What we need in our schools are experts who assist us to design high-quality assessments. We are finding that a difficult thing to do, yet it is so important." Teachers usually agree that assessments should be designed on the front end prior to designing strategies and activities, but that is just hard to do. That is why working through the skeleton unit first allows teachers to see what the end should look like.

Most teachers agree with the fundamental principle that assessment comes before strategies, but the majority of teachers with whom I have worked report that designing assessments and questions is easier said than done. That is why in the maps designed from skeleton units we use the student expectations to illustrate smaller steps toward the final student outcomes. Teachers experienced in designing final assessments may choose to do so, but it has been my experience that teachers appreciate that the incremental student expectations can substitute for the final assessment. Additionally, teachers report that by including the smaller steps, students can track their progress more easily.

The very nature of curriculum maps insists that they be somewhat brief. A hidden danger in this brevity is that it is possible to eliminate critical components of the map in order to keep the map from becoming too cumbersome for its intended audience of stakeholders—the students, the parents, other teachers, and the administrators. Maps that embed every critical component are sometimes so large that the reader or the audience loses interest. If maps include too much information, they trespass into the territory of skeleton units, yet if they contain too few critical components, they are no longer beneficial. Curriculum maps are frequently referred to as the road maps of learning, but if a road map included all of the intersecting streets, every shopping mall, church, grocery, school, dry cleaner, and gas station, then it would be too detailed to be effective over long distances. We do not want the details of what we have to pass to get to our destination unless those landmarks are important; we just want to easily see the pathway. Sometimes and in good faith, we include more than what is necessary in our maps or leave out critical parts. We teach students to identify their audience and purpose, and teachers who are developing a curriculum map should also keep that in mind when they decide what is critical to include in their maps.

Curriculum mapping is often touted as an effective and efficient method for helping teachers identify and eliminate the gaps and the unnecessary repetitions within their curriculum design. Although it is true that curriculum mapping really does enhance our ability to identify gaps, redundancies, and trends both horizontally and vertically, it is an extremely time-consuming endeavor. However, if we begin with the standards that are bundled and cross-bundled, then it becomes irrelevant because we take care of that issue on the front end of the process, thus saving possibly hundreds of hours of valuable time attending meetings to identify the gaps and unintentional repetitions. Curriculum maps can be created that have no gaps and only have repetitions that have been intentionally and purposefully included in the design. Collaborative groups examining these maps to identify trends, opportunities for additional integration, and possible resource and material conflicts will find the process less daunting and a more reasonable assignment if maps are scaffolded across and between grade levels and are free of gaps.

Formats for Curriculum Mapping

There are typically two types of formats for curriculum maps. The first is based on time such as a calendar map or other intervals of time within the school schedule such as semesters, school breaks, or quarters. The second type of format is based on the units or bundled standards. These maps reflect the natural breaks that occur as units reach closure.

Curriculum Maps Based on Time

A map based on the school calendar allows teachers to divide their curriculum or standards into monthly chunks of student learning. This organizational pattern is frequently seen at the primary and intermediate level. Since primary teachers often are responsible to embed the holidays into their curriculum framework, they frequently view a monthly map as the most practical way to organize for student learning and the holidays.

Another type of organization that is frequently used for curriculum mapping is one that is based on the quarters, six-week blocks, semesters, or some type of fixed interval. In these maps, teachers place their chunks of learning under the appropriate time period in which the content will be taught. For example, a teacher may organize his instruction into quarters to allow time for the closure of a unit prior to ending a grading period. Many middle and high school teachers favor this type of organization because it takes into consideration the natural breaks of grading, holidays, and in some cases final quarterly and semester exams.

There are several questions that teachers need to consider prior to settling on an organizational format based on time. First, will calendar mapping limit learning to only the predetermined chunks such as the study of African Americans only in the month of February, or will the rich contributions of African Americans be emphasized throughout the entire year as they should be? Are the topics of Native Americans and pilgrims always slated for the month of November because of Thanksgiving? Should the sequence of the curriculum be based on the calendar months, or on the developmental needs of students and the scaffolding of learning? Professional teachers giving consideration to these and other questions can make decisions that are in the students' best interest. For far too long, many schools have organized around what was the easiest method for the adults without putting the most important issue in the center of table—what is best for our students.

Some teachers insist on having maps divided into the calendar months because that is how they have seen other maps organized. If you have thoroughly considered all formats and decided to curriculum map using a monthly calendar design, arrange the curriculum based on how long each expectation and question will *probably* endure. However, be cautious not to fall into the trap of allowing the calendar to dictate the unit. Respect the natural curriculum breaks even when they happen in the middle of the month. A few brave teachers have confessed to lengthening or shortening a unit to make it fit their calendar.

Bundled Maps
Another way of designing curriculum maps centers on standards to be taught. As you will see, the maps designed from the process in this book are organized around the bundled and cross-bundled standards, which are our skeleton units. This process lends itself to curriculum mapping because it is based on the natural breaks in the curriculum rather than an arbitrary schedule or monthly blocks. A skeleton unit can easily be reorganized into a curriculum map, and it shouldn't take more than twenty to thirty minutes since all of the necessary elements have already been designed. What makes this format so different is that it is built from the length and design of the skeleton units, which are naturally within the standards instead of from an arbitrarily set time interval.

Mapping Is a By-Product, Not an End Product

A curriculum map should be developed using the standards to construct a pathway for student learning, just as a pathway was designed in the skeleton units. Teachers have little time to design an alignment document that does not serve a purpose, and a curriculum map is no exception. Teachers who map their curriculum need to know the best approach to the process so that after it is completed they don't have to sit through endless meetings searching for the gaps and unnecessary repetitions. By aligning and front-loading the standards into a curriculum map, valuable time is saved. But, be aware that just copying the standards into a map makes it way too long to be useful. In one school, teachers added all standards to each chunk of learning and their maps were so long that they threw them out and started over. That is why maps are developed based on the concepts and topics derived from the standards rather than including each individual standard.

Developing a curriculum map is simple if it begins with the examination of standards and proceeds to the development of a standards-based unit. Usually entire skeleton units are developed without stopping to create a curriculum map along the way. However, if a map is wanted, one can easily be created from this process.

Mapping Through the Skeleton Unit

Every teacher who develops a curriculum map brings to the table his or her own needs and wants. Some teachers want to see the concepts and topics while others will embed those within other components to make their maps more succinct. The possible elements that we have developed or identified during the creation of a skeleton unit are:

- Standards
- Umbrella concept
- Mutual umbrella expectations
- Umbrella questions
- Topics
- Essential content area expectations
- Essential questions
- Strategies
- Some possible guiding questions and activities

From this list, consider what you might include in your curriculum map to communicate a brief pathway without clogging the audience's senses with too much information. If you determine that guiding questions are essential, then the map could not be completed until lesson plans are fully developed since that is where the majority of the guiding questions have to be designed. If skills are essential, activities must be identified from the strategies, and final assessments must be fully developed before we can know all of the skills necessary for students.

Many teachers have trouble identifying which skills to include on a curriculum map as well as how and where to include them. It is a confusing proposition, and teachers frequently ask the following questions:

- Do I list all the skills students will use while studying this concept or topic or just the ones that students haven't mastered yet?

- Do I illustrate a link between the skills and the concepts, or do I just list them in a separate column or row?
- How can I know what skills my students will need before I know my students?
- Isn't it impossible to identify all the skills my students will need until I fully design my activities and continuous assessments?

The answer to all of these questions is not to include skills in a generic manner. If skills are included, only include those that are glaring such as a math standard that requires students to add two-digit numbers. Phrases such as "analyze the growth in the population of Africa over the last forty years" are too broad to be considered skills. Within that short phase many skills will eventually appear such as investigating, comparing, writing, graphing, and justifying. Discrete skills such as the math example are easy to identify; however, skills that only unfold through activities are impossible to include since lessons are not fully developed. Too many maps include skills that are not a realistic depiction of the eventual student activities and expectations.

When these types of questions were first encountered, answers were not readily available. However, the process of identifying and articulating student expectations later answered many of the teachers' concerns. The answer lies in the interpretation of skills. Thus, the use of skills is eliminated from our curriculum map and replaced with student expectations. These expectations have the skills embedded within the future strategies and activities silently waiting to be unveiled. For example, for the final expectation of "articulate the legacy of the government system in Rome," students might need the skill of summarizing, or they might need the skill of illustrating through a visual art project, which might include the skills of drawing, labeling, or measuring. Either way, until the activities are designed and until we assess the needs of our students, skills are hard to pinpoint.

Perhaps you have noticed by now that skills, final student expectations, strategies, and activities all use verbs to describe them. Because of their similar format, it is difficult for an outsider to delineate between them. The answer is usually in the intent of the person who designed it. Consider the following statement: "Interview a veteran to uncover little-known facts." Now, is that an activity, an assessment, or a skill? It could be any of these depending on its purpose. For example, it could be the final product because it might be videotaped and presented to the class, or it could be a skill where students learn the techniques of interviewing, or it could be an activity on the way to the final assessment of summarizing the interview. Only the author of that statement can define its purpose.

Examples of Curriculum Maps from Skeleton Units

Figure 6–1 is a map created from the middle school skeleton unit from Chapter 5. This map was developed in about twenty minutes by cutting and pasting elements from the skeleton unit into a map. The strands of science, social studies, and dance took merely two pages. By enlarging the paper, the other content areas such as math and language arts can be added and laid out side by side. Additionally, a larger piece of paper would allow the heading of the umbrella not to be repeated on each page so the entire map for all content areas can be displayed on a single page. This holds true most of the time. These types of maps are easily handled, displayed, and sent home to parents.

Examine Figure 6–1 and identify the following critical components that are included in this map:

- Umbrella questions
- Mutual umbrella expectations
- Essential questions
- Essential content area expectations

The umbrella concept of *systems* provided a thread that runs through the entire map in Figure 6–1. Additionally, notice that there are some topical connections between social studies and dance through the use of specific cultures such as Africa and China. Integration is alive and well in this map; however, it does not stop here. Teachers can now examine the big picture to locate other possible integration opportunities. Although not evident in this map, content areas can share the same essential questions, thus providing an additional intersecting point.

The curriculum map in Figure 6–1 does not have a separate column for assessments; rather, student expectations take the place of fully developed assessments. We know that every time an activity is designed we must pair it with a method for teachers to accurately monitor student progress. That is a big job, but it is how we continuously assess our students' progress. Teachers cannot possibly know if students are getting it if they are not intentionally monitoring.

We ask much of teachers without providing them appropriate training and practice time needed to master their new learning. Because teachers are

Systems: 7th Grade Curriculum Map

Umbrella Questions
- How do the parts of a system work together to perform a function?
- What can I predict about different systems based on investigations of their parts?

Mutual Umbrella Expectations
- Describe the structure of the parts and how they relate to the system.
- Describe the function of the parts and how they relate to the system.
- Justify the importance of various parts of a system.
- Provide evidence that parts and subsystems work together to create a system.
- Provide evidence and demonstrate how systems have been enhanced or improved through researching and studying their parts.

Science	Social Studies	Dance
Final Science Expectation for cells, tissue, organs, organ systems, and living systems • Students will be able to make predictions about their future based on their own investigations of factors that can affect cell systems. *Essential Questions and Science Expectations: What can I learn about my body by studying my parts?* • Articulate what you already know about systems. • Respond to umbrella questions. *How will I know a cell if I meet one?* • Articulate what you know about the system of the human body. • Explain with a thorough description the definition of a cell. • Identify animal cell parts. • Describe the structure and function of animal cell parts. • Compare and contrast animal and plant cell structures.	*Final Social Studies Expectations for social systems, political systems, economic systems, government systems in India, China, Africa, Ancient Greece, Ancient Rome* • Students will be able to justify how cultures are a system of beliefs, knowledge, institutions, traditions, and skills shared by a group. *Essential Questions and Social Studies Expectations: What systems can I identify in Ancient Rome, Greece, China, Africa, and India?* • Explain the systems of government, economic, social, and political. • Compare and contrast the economic systems of different cultures. • Provide evidence of the legacy of the systems of government from different cultures on your culture. • Identify key people within different cultures and explain their influence on that culture.	*Final Dance Expectations for movement and sequence, elements of dance, compositional form, expressional, culture, history, and social* • Create a dance with a beginning, middle, and end that communicates an idea using locomotor and nonlocomotor movement. *Essential Questions and Dance Expectations: How was the dance used by ancient cultures?* • Explain how dance has been a part of different cultures. • Articulate and provide evidence of the purposes of dance. • Compare and contrast how dances were used in different cultures: Africa China Ancient Rome Ancient Greece Native Americans Colonial Americans India

FIGURE 6–1. Middle School Standards-Based Curriculum Map

continued

Science	Social Studies	Dance
• Describe observations of an animal cell and plant cell using a microscope. • Provide evidence of the essential elements of cell theory. • Understand the structures and functions in an animal cell. *How do systems in my body work together most efficiently in order to sustain life?* • Compare and contrast single-celled and multicelluar organisms. • Identify differences among specialized cells (nerve, muscle, blood, skin, bone). • Explain how cells have specialized functions and work together to form the levels of organization (cells, tissues, organs, organ system, organism). • Explain how different cell processes function in order to sustain life (diffusion, osmosis, respiration, photosynthesis, reproduction, mitosis). • Evaluate the importance of how different systems in a cell work together to perform cell process. *How have discoveries about cells affected me?* • Evaluate the importance of a body system in relation to the organism. • Explain the effects of current cell research on diseases and treatment options. • Predict what your future life will be like if cell research continues to improve treatment options.	*What can I learn about different cultures by studying their systems?* • Analyze key influences such as art and beliefs as they relate to each culture. • How do the political, economic, and social systems work together? • Provide evidence that the political, economic, and social systems in different cultures affected each other. *How do discoveries from ancient cultures shape my beliefs about these civilizations?* • Design artifacts that would represent each different culture and analyze actual artifacts to determine how they reflect each culture.	*How can I communicate using the elements of dance?* • Compare and contrast dance movements with movements made in daily life. • Use locomotor movements (walk, run, skip, hop, jump, slide, leap, gallop) to create a simple dance. • Create a dance using nonlocomotor movements (bend, stretch, twist, swing) that portray the feelings of a chosen culture. *How was space and energy used in different cultures?* • Create a dance using space, time, and force to depict a chosen culture. • Articulate by using appropriate terminology the differences and similarities in different dances. *How can I change the movements and the time within a dance to reflect a different culture?* • Create and perform a dance depicting a chosen culture and use the elements of dance with locomotor and nonlocomotor movements.

Source: Susan Walker, Teresa Haynes, Nolan Sanders, Janet Miles, and Gayla Martin, Olmstead Middle School, 2002–2003.

FIGURE 6–1. *continued*

busy professionals with too much in their laps, the map in Figure 6–1 uses student expectations to nudge teachers to think ahead rather than to force teachers to design a final assessment that is based on very little substance and is very likely to change. To illustrate the potential pitfall, look at the following example. This is an excerpt from a map developed by teachers who were not provided appropriate training.

CONTENT	SKILLS	ASSESSMENTS
Civil War	Note-taking	Oral presentations
Immigration	Reading	Teacher observation
Reconstruction	Conducting interview	Open response question
	Generating questions	Debate

Can you tell by looking at this example when debate would be used as an assessment? Do you remember taking tests that required that a line be drawn between items with a relationship or a significant link? These types of tests were usually called *matching*. To see the match between the skills, the content, and the assessments in this example, a line linking them would need to be included. This is one of the inherent dangers in turning a curriculum map into a list of items. By using the essential questions and the essential content area expectations, we can sequence our maps into a strategic progression of scaffolding learning.

Figure 6–2 is an actual primary curriculum map. The simple design of the map provides a pathway that is easy for all teachers to understand. The student expectations are sequenced so that learning is scaffolded. Teachers designed this map from their previous work and it took very little time. Even they were amazed at how easy the process was. The teachers discovered by viewing this holistic map that they were not happy with some of their questions so they are exploring ways to make them more interesting to students. They view this map as continuously under construction. Therefore, Figure 6–2 is a beginning map in progress, which is the way it should be.

The final example in Figure 6–3 is a high school map that integrates three content areas. By looking at all three maps (Figures 6–1 through 6–3), it is evident that developing curriculum is the same for all grade levels. Educators tend to think that high schools are so different that what happens at the elementary level is not applicable to the secondary level. The map in Figure 6–3 proves how wrong that assumption is.

Although the departmental configuration in high schools often limits the number of content areas that are included in a curriculum map, map-

Umbrella Concept: Relationships

Umbrella Statement: To understand how things are connected and relate to our lives.

Umbrella Question: How am I connected?

Mutual Umbrella Expectations
- Identify relationships in which students are a part.
- Solve problems within relationships.
- Compare and contrast how things are related.

Social Studies	Science	Math	Writing	The Arts
Native Americans Colonial Americans • Celebrations • Dress • Home • Food • Transportation • Government • Family roles and responsibilities *Essential Question* • How are my customs different from yours?	Motion Force Push Pull Energy Heat Light Sound *Essential Question* • How can understanding the laws of motion and force make my life easier than yours? *Essential Science Expectations* • Know and understand motion and force.	Fact families (skip count by two) Problem solving Time Money *Essential Question* • How can I use number relationships to help solve problems? *Essential Math Expectations* • Understand fact families. • Illustrate the relationship between fact families.	Writing process Short stories Transactive writing Literary elements Reflections Connections to real life Predicting/conclusion *Essential Question* • How can what I read and write connect me to the world?	Sound Music Culture Musical elements Music of Native Americans, Colonial Americans, and various other cultures *Essential Question* • How will I know if you hear what I hear?

continued

FIGURE 6–2. Primary Curriculum Map: Relationships

Social Studies	Science	Math	Writing	The Arts
Essential Social Studies Expectations • Articulate the customs of Native Americans. • Compare and contrast how customs are alike and different. • Demonstrate customs and beliefs of Native Americans. *Essential Question* • How are my customs different from yours? *Essential Social Studies Expectations* • Articulate the customs of Colonial Americans. • Compare and contrast how customs are alike and different. • Demonstrate customs and beliefs of Colonial Americans.	• Design an invention demonstrating the relationship between motion and force. *Essential Question* • How is my relationship with energy different than your relationship? *Essential Science Expectations* • Understand how heat, light, and sound travels. • Demonstrate how heat, light, and sound are produced. • Predict/hypothesize the reaction of light, heat, and sound in different situations.	• Solve problems using relationships. *Essential Question* • How is time important to me? *Essential Math Expectations* • Identify time to the different increments. • Demonstrate the relationship between calendar and time as it applies to me. *Essential Question* • How is money important to me? *Essential Math Expectations* • Identify money to the different increments. • Demonstrate the relationship between different denominations.	*Essential Writing Expectations* • Use text elements to understand what you read. • Demonstrate connections to what is read to real life. • Make predictions. • Draw conclusions. • Use text elements to enhance writing. • Apply the writing process. • Develop well-organized and detailed ideas to relate to the audience.	*Essential Music Expectations* • Understand the role of music in and its relationship to different cultures such as Native American, Colonial American, and other various cultures. • Classify music by its elements • Compare and contrast various types of music.

Source: Chandlers School Map Primary Map (P2/3). Created by Belle Rush, Lana Whitaker, Kim Grise, and Shanna Willen, 2002–2003.

FIGURE 6–2. *continued*

Systems: 11th Grade Curriculum Map

Umbrella Questions
- How can I use a system to my benefit?
- How can I modify a system?

Mutual Umbrella Expectations
- Identify systems that have protocols.
- Justify the importance of a variety of systems.
- Create a set of protocols for a system.
- Provide evidence and justify why it is important to modify and use systems.

Science	English/Oral Communication	Math
Final Science Expectation for measurement, metric system, accuracy, precision • Students will be able to apply and manipulate the metric system in making measurements and calculating accuracy and precision. *Essential Question* • What makes the metric system different from the U.S. Standard system? *Essential Science Expectations* • Articulate what you already know about the two measurement systems. • Respond to umbrella questions. *Essential Question* • How do I apply the terminology involved with the metric system to represent my measurements? *Essential Science Expectations* • Identify eight most common prefixes used in labeling units of the metric system. • Explain the justification for using Latin and Greek prefixes over English or French.	*Final English/Oral Communication Expectation for presentation speaking, debate format, research of issue, investigating both sides of an issue, persuasive argumentation* • Students will be able to research, prepare, and deliver arguments, justifications, and rebuttals regarding a resolution related to the use of the metric system. *Essential Question* • How can I design a good debate? *Essential English Expectations* • Identify the components of debate procedure. • Compare and contrast the advantages and disadvantages of the speaking order of both affirmative and negative sides. • Explain why the protocol for debates is important to use. *Essential Question* • What can I learn from preparing for a debate argument?	*Final Math Expectation for metric conversion, calculation of accuracy and precision* • Students will be able to convert measurements within both systems of measurement and calculate appropriate relationships in terms of accuracy and precision. *Essential Questions* • What does accuracy represent? • How can I calculate accuracy? *Essential Math Expectations* • Explain how accuracy measurements affect consumer confidence in products. (social studies connection) • Evaluate appropriate levels of accuracy in regard to a given situation. • Articulate and provide evidence of the relative ease of use in calculating accuracy with metric system units. *Essential Questions* • What does precision represent? • How can I calculate precision?

FIGURE 6–3. High School Standards-Based Curriculum Map

continued

Science	English/Oral Communication	Math
• Compare and contrast the relative ease of recognizing metric system values from reading the written term. *Essential Question* • What practical applications of the metric system can I use in present-day United States? *Essential Science Expectations* • Identify ten examples of items measured in the metric system commonly used in the United States. • Theorize why some of the listed items have transcended tradition and marketed themselves metrically instead of the standard system. • Hypothesize three items that logically could be the next items to be marketed in metric quantities. • Evaluate the importance of using metrically measured products in the United States. *Essential Question* • Where are precision and accuracy important in the real world? *Essential Science Expectations* • Provide evidence of the use of precision and accuracy measurements. • Explain the effect of providing this type of measurement. • Predict what your future life would be like if either accuracy or precision values were not followed.	*Essential English Expectations* • Articulate and provide evidence for the benefits of researching both sides of the issue. • Analyze how growth potentials in public speaking, persuasive argumentation, and a respectful protocol can be of use in future careers. *Essential Question* • How will I know the difference between speaking during a debate from other types of speech? *Essential English Expectations* • Compare and contrast debate presentations with a persuasive speech. • Analyze the aspects of debate in terms of presentation versus content and their relative importance to a successful debate.	*Essential Math Expectations* • Explain how precision measurements directly or indirectly affect our economy. • Evaluate appropriate levels of precision in regard to a given situation. • Articulate and provide evidence of the relative ease of use in calculating precision with metric system units. *Essential Question* • How can I make conversions from within the metric system? *Essential Math Expectations* • Manipulate unit conversion from within the metric system sans calculator. • Compare/contrast relative ease of unit conversion between standard and metric systems. *Essential Question* • How can I make conversions between metric and standard systems? *Essential Math Expectations* • Articulate the process of using conversion factors to successfully convert from one system to another. • Explain the importance of being able to convert between systems.

Source: Created by Jeremy Brown and Kris-Anne Ferguson, Logan County High School, 2003.

FIGURE 6–3. *continued*

ping is also a process that can be accomplished for one content area or several together. In the high school map, Jeremy Brown and Kris-Anne Ferguson worked collaboratively to create connections that crossed barriers that are usually considered impassable.

Using a Map to Communicate

Curriculum maps can be useful communication tools. Teachers are always finding new and exciting ways to use maps to communicate. In one school, teachers have enlarged their maps to the size of a poster and laminated them. Each time a student expectation is introduced, it is circled on the enlarged map and referred to as students work toward that goal. In this way, the curriculum map assists students to see where they are going and what they have accomplished. Other teachers share that a curriculum map, because of its inherent brevity, is perfect for taking to meetings and distributing to parents, students, and colleagues.

Pitfalls to Avoid

If we view curriculum mapping as final goal, then we may never get to the development of a standards-based unit. This is a trap that many schools, districts, and even some states have fallen prey to. In other words, curriculum maps are not an end product or goal. They are an oasis on the road to designing a pathway for students. They often provide a resting spot, a pit stop, or a place to spend the night, but they are never the final destination. Figure 6–4 illustrates that a curriculum map naturally falls out of the process outlined in this book prior to developing strategies for our skeleton unit.

Educators who see curriculum mapping as an end product and who judge schools and teachers by whether they have a curriculum map are hindering those who see beyond curriculum mapping and into a future rich with possibilities. It is easy to get caught up in the curriculum mapping frenzy and forget that curriculum maps and standards-based units go hand-in-hand. Indeed, a curriculum map is nothing more than a by-product along the pathway of building a standards-based unit.

Summing Up

Although the process outlined in this book is not the only pathway to an aligned curriculum or to the development of standards-based units and curriculum maps, it is a pathway created by practicing educators who are under

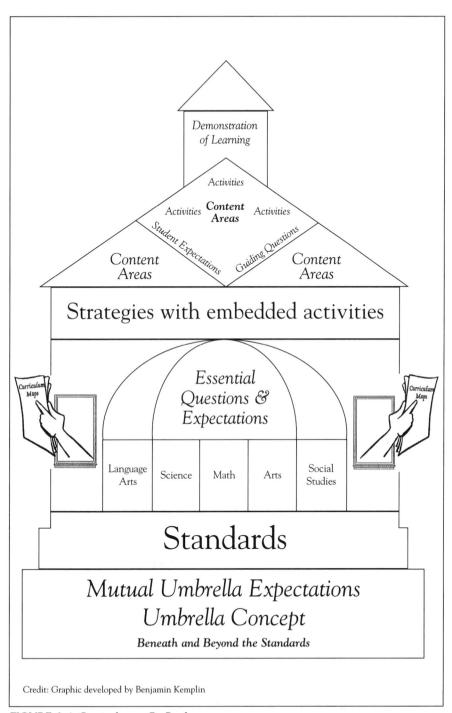

Demonstration
of Learning

Activities

Activities **Content Areas** Activities

Student Expectations   Guiding Questions

Content
Areas

Content
Areas

Strategies with embedded activities

Curriculum Maps

Curriculum Maps

Essential
Questions &
Expectations

| Language Arts | Science | Math | Arts | Social Studies |

Standards

Mutual Umbrella Expectations
Umbrella Concept
Beneath and Beyond the Standards

Credit: Graphic developed by Benjamin Kemplin

FIGURE 6–4. Curriculum as By-Product

intense pressure to assist their students to score higher on state-mandated tests. The process took years to develop with many failures and mistakes along the way. In fact, the process itself will always be evolving. Most important, though, is that the process brings about real change in the language of teachers. Morgantown Elementary School Assistant Principal Vonda Jennings said, "Our work with bundling standards and identifying how they can be used to teach to a higher level was the best professional development we have ever had. Teachers talked to each other more and in a different language during that process and almost a year later, we are still using that language and our products to guide our instruction."

It has been my experience that this process can bring about change in a school, and it can help students achieve at higher levels. As with any journey, teachers need the support of each other and of the administration while working to construct a pathway for students. But many teachers have told me that if they lost their units, no one could take away what they learned during the process. I have seen, as have hundreds of teachers, that the process itself is as important as the products that it produces.

Terms to Remember

Curriculum Maps: A way to organize the curriculum into specific chunks of learning either by the school calendar, other time intervals, or the natural breaks in the curriculum.

Further Reading

Barr, M. A., D. A. Craig, D. Fisette, and M. A. Syverson. 1999. *Assessing Literacy with the Learning Record: A Handbook for Teachers, Grades K–6*. Portsmouth, NH: Heinemann.

Barr, M. A., M. A. Syverson, and A. McKittrick. 1999. *Assessing Literacy with the Learning Record: A Handbook for Teachers, Grades 6–12*. Portsmouth, NH: Heinemann.

Hein, G. E., and S. Price. 1994. *Active Assessment for Active Science: A Guide for Elementary School Teachers*. Portsmouth, NH: Heinemann.

Jacobs, H. H. 1997. *Mapping the Big Picture: Integrating Curriculum and Assessment K–12*. Alexandria, VA: ASCD.

Kuhs, T. M. 1997. *Measure for Measure: Using Portfolios in K–8 Mathematics*. Portsmouth, NH: Heinemann.

Mahoney, J., and J. Strickland. 2002. *Power and Portfolios: Best Practices for*

High School Classrooms. Portsmouth, NH: Heinemann.

Owocki, G., and Y. Goodman. 2002. *Kidwatching: Documenting Children's Literacy Development*. Portsmouth, NH: Heinemann.

Wiggins, G. 1998. *Educative Assessment: Designing Assessments to Inform and Improve Student Performance*. San Francisco, CA: Jossey-Bass

Wiggins, G., and J. McTighe. 1999. *The Understanding by Design Handbook*. Alexandria, VA: ASCD.

APPENDIX A
BUNDLING STANDARDS

Standard # and Content Area	Standards	Bundle Titles			

APPENDIX B
CONCEPT WORKSHEET

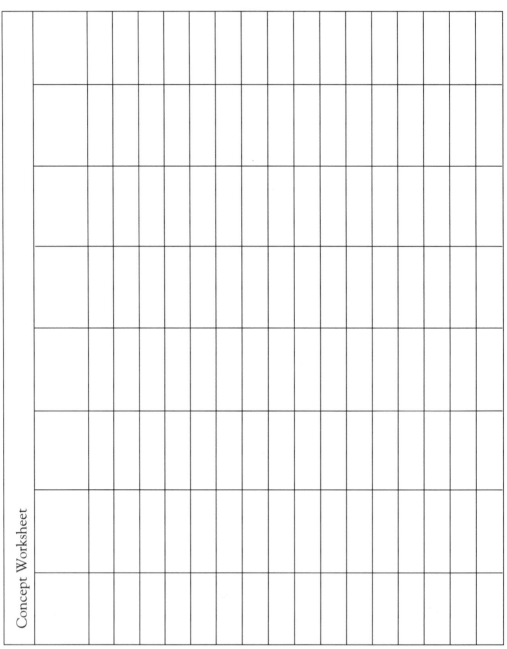

Concept Worksheet

APPENDIX C
CURRICULUM MAP

Umbrella Concept:
Umbrella Questions:
Mutual Umbrella Expectations:

Final Expectations	Final Expectations	Final Expectations	Final Expectations	Final Expectations	Final Expectations
Essential Questions and Content Area Expectations	Essential Questions and Content Area Expectations	Essential Questions and Content Area Expectations	Essential Questions and Content Area Expectations	Essential Questions and Content Area Expectations	Essential Questions and Content Area Expectations

Learning Link: Activating, Assessing, Eliminating, Engaging
Umbrella Concept:
Umbrella Questions (Hook)
Mutual Umbrella Expectations 1. 2. 3.
Final Content Expectation
Essential Content Expectations 1. 2. 3. 4. 5.
Concepts:
Topics:
Essential Questions (Hook) 1. 2.
Student Strategies 1. 2. 3. 4. 5.
Approximate Timeline

Persistent Exploration

Essential Questions (Hook)

Possible Guiding Questions

Essential Content Learning

Essential Content Expectations

1.

2.

3.

4.

5.

Concepts:

Topics:

Student Strategies
1.

2.

3.

4.

5.

6.

Approximate Timeline

Learning Link: Internalizing, Reflecting, Connecting, Extending

Essential Questions (Hook)

Possible Guiding Questions

Essential Content Learning

Essential Content Expectations

1.

2.

3.

4.

5.

Concepts:

Topics:

Student Strategies

1.

2.

3.

4.

5.

6.

Approximate Timeline